Adapting

Adapting Graham Greene

RICHARD J. HAND

and

ANDREW PURSSELL

First published 2015 by
PALGRAVE

Palgrave in the UK is an imprint of Macmillan Publishers Limited, registered in England, company number 785998, of 4 Crinan Street, London N1 9XW.

Palgrave Macmillan in the US is a division of St Martin's Press LLC, 175 Fifth Avenue, New York, NY 10010.

Palgrave is a global imprint of the above companies and is represented throughout the world.

Palgrave® and Macmillan® are registered trademarks in the United States, the United Kingdom, Europe and other countries.

ISBN 978-0-230-57904-0   ISBN 978-1-137-49157-2 (eBook)

DOI 10.1007/978-1-137-49157-2

This book is printed on paper suitable for recycling and made from fully managed and sustained forest sources. Logging, pulping and manufacturing processes are expected to conform to the environmental regulations of the country of origin.

A catalogue record for this book is available from the British Library.

A catalog record for this book is available from the Library of Congress.

Typeset by MPS Limited, Chennai, India.

Contents

Acknowledgements

This study benefitted considerably from discussions with colleagues in the School of Drama and Music at the University of South Wales, the Department of English at Royal Holloway, University of London (in particular Robert Hampson), and at the *Journal of Adaptation in Film and Performance*. The authors would also like to thank Gill Allard and Brett Mills for commissioning this book and Nicola Cattini for her patient support during its preparation. The authors wish to express particular gratitude to the staff at the British Film Institute Library, London, for their helpful guidance through the Greene materials held in their Special Collections, to Andrew Glazzard (Royal Holloway) for the invitation to speak at the Adapting Conrad Conference at the Institute of English Studies in 2014, where some of the issues explored in this study were first aired, and to the Graham Greene Birthplace Trust for the award of a small research grant and, beyond this, much friendly encouragement besides.

Introduction

Adaptation – whereby a source text is taken and is translated into a different form – has been for centuries a common cultural practice, and is arguably a central process in Western culture as a whole. To this end, we might consider the use of the oral tradition in the formation of classical Greek dramatic texts, or the dramatization of Scripture into medieval miracle and mystery plays. If we take the preeminent figure of English Literature – William Shakespeare – we find an adapter *par excellence*. Shakespeare uses a wide range of sources to inspire, influence or underpin his dramatic works, including the plays of the Roman writers Plautus and Seneca, the history books of Plutarch (in Thomas North's translation) and Holinshed, as well as the works of numerous other (usually Italian) authors. Looked at from this angle, we soon realize that the perceived greatness of Shakespeare lies less in his 'originality', than in his exceptional ability to conglomerate and re-apply materials and models in the creation of new dramatic works. However, Shakespeare's points of textual origin are not, in themselves, definitive or stable. As Linda Hutcheon notes, Shakespeare's *Romeo and Juliet* (c. 1597) is an adaptation of 'Arthur Brooke's versification of Matteo Bandello's adaptation of Luigi da Porto's version of Masuccio Salernitano's story' (Hutcheon, 2006, p. 177). Moreover, just as Shakespeare was an adapter, so, too, have his plays been transformed, in turn, into a countless number of reinterpretations, appropriations and intertextual allusions throughout history and across different cultures. As all of this suggests, the origins and endpoints of Shakespeare, as an arch adapter himself and as an author whose works will continue to be adapted through the centuries, are open and ongoing.

There are countless examples of adaptation in the history of English theatre in the centuries after Shakespeare. By the nineteenth and early-twentieth century the novel was the dominant literary form in Britain, and novels provided ready subject matter for stage

1

dramatizations. The hugely popular Victorian playhouses featured dramatizations of contemporary novels as a staple genre, and this was due in no small part to the flawed copyright laws of the period, which left novelists unprotected from adaptation: a novel could be published, dramatized for the stage, but without any remuneration for the original novelist (unless they themselves wrote their own stage version). Attending this issue of economic worth were questions of 'literary value': the resulting melodramas may have been immensely popular, but they were disparaged by those who wanted to see the renaissance of an English literary theatre which would return the English stage to the status and quality they believed it demonstrated in the era of Shakespeare. In other words, and despite its central importance in Shakespeare, adaptation was seen to be somehow damaging to the national literature. Nevertheless, their popular appeal underlines a central commonplace of adaptation, then as now: that a 'good story' is not only worth re-reading but also re-telling and re-interpreting in new and different ways. The dramatization of literary fiction continued undiminished over the turn of the twentieth century and, in an interesting phenomenon in English literary history, major novelists of the period such as Henry James, Thomas Hardy and Joseph Conrad were encouraged to become playwrights themselves, frequently choosing their own novels as source texts – albeit with less than triumphant results. After all, although adaptation may have been ubiquitous, it does not follow that it is easy.

In recent years, international academics such as Deborah Cartmell, Imelda Whelehan, Robert Stam, Linda Hutcheon, Julie Sanders and Thomas Leitch have helped to create and consolidate the field of Adaptation Studies, as the study of adaptation has grown from being a niche within literary, film or cultural studies, into a scholarly field in its own right. In her enlightening account of the rise and prolific growth of Adaptation Studies, Márta Minier discusses the terminology of 'adaptation' as a cultural process in relation to other affiliated – and occasionally synonymous – terms such as appropriation, translation, transformation, allusion and intertextuality (Minier, 2014, p. 15). In addition, there are further terms which are sub-generic or generically more specific, including parodies, imitations, spinoffs, offshoots and 'tradaptations' (Minier, 2014, p. 16), and which encompass a variety of attitudes that can be as reverential as 'homage', as unscrupulous as 'rip-off' or as scurrilous as 'send-up'. As all of this suggests, adaptation is a broad field. But what all these terms have in common is a core process whereby a source text (in the broadest sense of the term) is taken and 'reworked' or 'turned into' another text. In her definition of adaptation as an act which signals 'a relationship with an informing source text or original' (Sanders, 2006, p. 26), Julie Sanders reveals just how all-encompassing the process of adaptation can be and gestures to its impact in other media. For example, adaptation is an important practice not just in the world of theatre but also of radio. As a new performance medium which burgeoned alongside the development of sound cinema in the 1920s, radio drama began as an art form specializing in adaptation (initially of stage plays and then of literary fiction), and adaptation remains a core element in modern radio programming: above all, BBC radio has been a world leader in audio adaptation, habitually exploring the rich seams of world literature to bring celebrated classics as well as more neglected works to the attention of its listeners. Beyond this, our own time has seen an exponential proliferation of adaptations across the widest range of cultural productions: theatre, radio, television, graphic art and even digital games are distinct forms of performance media which include adaptation as a central genre and practice.

Although adaptation is a process which occurs across the fullest range of cultures and media, it is perennially evident that adaptation has a special place and connotation in the world of cinema, centring in particular on the conversion of narrative fiction into film. The reflex association of adaptation with cinema is not without good reason: the screen industries of film and television have, after all, made adaptation a central enterprise. Underpinning this is cinema's quest for a 'good narrative': something which will attract, and secure, the attention – and money – of an audience over tens, and often hundreds, of minutes of screen time; this is where cinema's interest in novels – as vehicles of extended narrative – and their authors – has come from. For although many celebrated novelists are distinguished by their skills in literary effect and technique, the core interest for the mainstream cinema industry is the *stories* which lie at the heart of their works. Narrative is at the centre of cinematic practice: the function of *mise-en-scène*, design, music and effects in conventional cinema has been to assist and fulfil the telling of a story over time, on screen. This book will concentrate on cinema. Although the focal-point of this study, Graham Greene, is a writer whose works have appealed to radio, television and theatre, it is cinema with which his name will forever be associated. This association has led to a body of work which could be viewed as its own subgenre of screen adaptation: *Cinematic Greene*.

As we will see, Greene's own prolonged and at times symbiotic relationship with cinema makes this a subgenre that is as complex as it is compelling.

Adaptation is very much an umbrella term which encompasses numerous genres and subgenres within cinema, just as it straddles different media. Examples include fact-based dramatizations such as biographical works (or 'biopics', one of the most popular and, frequently, critically acclaimed genres in mainstream cinema), pastiches and parodies (or 'spoofs'), musical versions, and so on. This should perhaps come as no surprise: from Daniel Defoe's pseudo-autobiographical adaptation of the 'real-life' tale of Alexander Selkirk, *Robinson Crusoe* (1719), to *Shamela* (1741), Henry Fielding's comedic re-imagining of Samuel Richardson's *Pamela* (1740), the biography and the parody together form part of the foundation of the modern novel, a genre which in turn lies at the heart of screen adaptation. In addition, certain types of film releases, such as remakes, sequels and prequels, can themselves be considered examples of adaptation. Yet another level of adaptation concerns the marketing and merchandising of film franchises with cross-media processes that encompass promotional clothing, posters and 'books of the film', as well as video games and theme park rides based on films. Closing the loop of this möbius strip of adaptation, there are even examples of films that have grown out from the worlds of toy manufacture and the theme park, such as the incredibly popular (and high-grossing) *Transformers* (2007—) and *Pirates of the Caribbean* (2003—) franchises.

As all of this suggests, adaptation has an acute significance in the history of cinema. Although the beginnings of cinema as a medium are contested, the Auguste and Louis Lumière film screenings in Paris in 1895 are usually taken as marking the inauguration of the cinema age. In the first years after the invention of the motion picture, the medium was seen as having primarily a 'scientific' use, fulfilling what we would today see as a 'documentary' function. Soon after this, cinema began producing short entertainments, playful novelties and comic sketches. After 1907, however, cinema had begun to outgrow its scientific and 'novelty' statuses, and there was an increasing demand (especially in the United States) for more sophisticated narratives: as Eileen Bowser points out, the adaptation of literary works provided a ready solution (Bowser, 1990, pp. 42–3). Accordingly, the early US film industry was fed by a spate of Shakespeare adaptations in 1908, followed by one-reel versions of Goethe's *Faust* (1909), Dickens's *A Christmas Carol* (1910), Lewis Carroll's *Alice's Adventures in*

Wonderland (1910) and Mary Shelley's *Frankenstein* (1910), all produced by Edison Studios, owned by the American inventor Thomas Edison.

The rise of the new medium was attended by a rising moral panic. Cinema was an irresistible target for those seeking a root cause for the social issues which characterized the newly arrived twentieth century. As Guy Phelps puts it: 'the cinema [was] blamed for almost every social calamity of the preceding decade' (Phelps, 1997, p. 62). In the United States, Edison warned in 1907 that the success and future of the cinema industry depended upon it establishing a 'good moral tone' (Bowser, 1990, p. 37). In Britain meanwhile, the 1909 Cinematograph Act was passed ostensibly to safeguard the physical environment of buildings where highly inflammable films were exhibited. Yet the passing of this Act also marked the beginnings of film censorship: the would-be protectors of film also wanted to protect audiences from its 'corrupting' effects. It was with this threat to its early existence in mind that cinema moved to protect itself through adaptation, by looking to confer upon itself 'the prestige of the classics' of literature (Bowser, 1990, p. 43).

There are a number of other reasons for the proliferation of screen adaptations. On one level, it reflects a cautious film industry that is reluctant to take chances on original, and thereby untested, storylines. A published source text which has been a commercial or critical success, on the other hand, offered a ready-made story and the promise of box-office success. It is with this in mind that Hollywood has over the years spent extraordinary sums buying up the rights to works of popular fiction, creating enormously popular franchises out of Marvel comics or J. K. Rowling's *Harry Potter* novels, to identify two of the most notable current examples of this proliferation. Moreover, in practices that reveal the inherent cynicism of the film industry, Hollywood can also be found securing film rights to novels before they have even been published, or buying the rights to a novel with no immediate intention other than to prevent other, rival film companies from producing their own film version. In this way, adaptation can be seen to have destructive as well as creative ends.

In addition to these financial motivations, the film industry has long attempted to prove its artistic credentials by investing in a 'prestige' adaptation, with numerous examples of literary fiction (both classic and contemporary) underpinning acclaimed and award-winning films. Sometimes the title of a successful novel is enough to secure the interest of audiences whose enjoyment of the original made it a popular success in the first place, or which have not read the book but have been waiting for the inevitable film version. The same is true of popular authors, and adaptations of novels by Jane Austen, Charles Dickens and E. M. Forster have become subgenres of cinema in their own right. Frequently, these films do little to hide their original sources, but instead foreground the names of their long-dead authors in much the same way they do the names of their leading actors. Indeed, the names of such classic authors have, in themselves, a cachet that continues to have popular appeal, aesthetic value and – for adaptors – the potential for profit and acclaim. At the same time, not all films are as open about their sources, just as one film may be an *overt* adaptation, another might be a *hidden* adaptation.

For instance, Alfred Hitchcock continues to be regarded as one of the great *auteurs* of cinema whose works are milestones of influence and originality. Throughout his long career, however, Hitchcock habitually produced adaptations of literary fiction: sometimes this adaptive process was overt, as with films such as *The Lodger* (1927), *The 39 Steps* (1935) and *Rebecca* (1940), based on the hugely popular novels by Marie Belloc Lowndes, John Buchan and Daphne du Maurier, respectively. At other times, this was less so: it is not made immediately apparent to audiences that *Vertigo* (1958), *Psycho* (1960) and *The Birds* (1963) find their sources in literary works by Boileau-Narcejac, Robert Bloch and, again, du Maurier (albeit one of her less-known works). Of these 'hidden' adaptations, some had particularly disguised origins. When buying the rights to Bloch's *Psycho* (1959), Hitchcock kept his identity firmly a secret, and this enabled him to secure them for a mere $9500; the subsequent film (made for less than a million dollars) would become the highest-grossing film up to that point in cinema history. In his hunger to acquire source novels, Hitchcock was not always incognito, and neither did the books even have to be in print: Hitchcock was keen to own the film rights to Greene's *Our Man in Havana* (1958), trying to secure these before the book had been published or, as Greene's letters suggest, even finished. Greene, never a fan of Hitchcock's work, flatly refused and the 1959 film version was a completely separate project made by Carol Reed. Hitchcock, for his part, went on to film another tale of Cold War espionage, *North by Northwest* (1959), and this became – in stark contrast to Reed's *Our Man in Havana* – an abiding favourite of critics and audiences.

In this context of reception, it is briefly worth considering the place of cinematic adaptation in the Academy of Motion Picture

Arts and Sciences Awards (better known as the 'Oscars'). Since the mid-twentieth century, there have been two categories for screenplays: the Academy Award for Best Writing (Original Screenplay) and the Academy Award for Best Writing (Adapted Screenplay). The lists of awards for the former category make interesting reading as they frequently contain works that owe a considerable debt to pre-extant textual sources, as well as scripts of unalloyed 'originality'. By the same token, those for the latter category often reveal debts to source texts that have otherwise been obscured, as well as examples of adaptations that overtly display their origins. An interesting recent example is the multi-Oscar-winning film *Slumdog Millionaire* (Danny Boyle, 2008), the acclaim surrounding which tended – at least in the West – to overlook that it was based on Vikas Swarup's 2005 novel *Q & A*.

The context of reception is a freighted one in adaptation studies. Frequently, an adaptation is held to be inherently derivative, and thereby inferior, because of its temporal location in the line of production: for some, adaptation is suggestive merely of the 'secondhand'. If some adaptations can be seen as 'cashing in' on their literary foundations, others find it difficult to live up to the reputation of their source. For instance, the film *Atonement* (Joe Wright, 2007) may have been critically acclaimed, but it was rare to find a review that did not mention Ian McEwan's 2001 source novel. At the most basic level of reception in adaptation is the commonplace that the film pales in comparison with the book on which it is based. However, even a cursory examination of this cliché reveals an essential truth that should always be kept in view when exploring adaptation more broadly: namely, that fiction and film are different forms and media created in different ways, in different contexts, and with different purposes in mind. As obvious as this may sound, we should always remember this before falling prey to the reductive and simplistic value judgement that 'the book is always better'. Rather, we should remind ourselves that books and films are fundamentally different from one another, a fact which takes on a particular resonance when it comes to the loaded issue of *fidelity*. Often, an appraisal of an adaptation becomes a discussion of how far a film has – or has not – been 'faithful' to the source text, and this can appear to relegate the adaptation to a lower moral plane – as does the commonplace that a given film is 'not *as good* as the book'. When the two are combined, film is put in a terminally inferior position. As Thomas M. Leitch eloquently puts it: 'Like translations to a new language, adaptations will always reveal their sources' superiority because whatever their faults, the source texts will always be better at being themselves' (Leitch, 2003, p. 161).

At the same time, however, and however different these appear as media, there are essential similarities between them. As the Russian Formalists and their counterparts in Britain and America, the New Critics, posited, a text can be viewed as directly presenting the reader with a *plot*, at the heart of which is a unifying, concrete *story*. In all but the most experimental examples, novels and films have, at their heart, a story. This story is unfurled through the mechanics of narrative and plot, and is conveyed by the words on the page and the frames on the screen. In the case of an adaptation, the story told by a novel and by the film of that novel is shared, although the medium is totally different.

When comparing an adaptation with its source, it can be helpful to look closely at the transformation of the *shared stories* – the common ground of all of the adaptations of Greene's works explored over the coming chapters. When looking at a novel and the subsequent film version of it, we can map out the adaptive process using these 'Five Creative Strategies of Adaptation' (Hand, 2010, p. 17):

- Omission
- Addition
- Marginalization
- Expansion
- Alteration

Film adaptations tend to use *omission* as their predominant strategy. For obvious reasons, a film cannot include every detail presented in the novel on which it is based without being prohibitively long in duration: we might expect to devote many hours (rarely in one sitting) in reading a novel, whereas we typically expect a film to be a much more focused experience (usually in one sitting). To this end a film will tend to omit or even conflate certain characters, scenes and subplots, in order to streamline and adapt the narrative to its practical needs as a medium – as we will see, for example, with Rowan Joffe's 2010 adaptation of Greene's 1938 novel *Brighton Rock*. A less common strategy is the use of *addition*: that is, where characters or incidents not in the source text are introduced in the adaptation, as we will see, for instance, with Neil Jordan's 1999 adaptation of Greene's 1951 novel *The End of the Affair*. Often this is to do with the generic expectations, and the limits to representation, of each medium. For example, an action sequence might be introduced that will function particularly well in the visual and intrinsically dynamic context of film (after all, a car chase is probably less interesting on the page than it is on the big screen, much in the same way that the narrative stream-of-consciousness of James Joyce or Virginia Woolf does not easily lend itself to the screen). With regard to *marginalization*, central themes or incidents in a novel may be made less important than they are in the original novel or are simply alluded to. Conversely, with regard to *expansion*, seemingly minor details in a novel can be made to appear more significant or pivotal in the screen version. Finally, the strategy of *alteration* describes the process whereby geographical or historical settings or characters – or even storylines and endings – are radically changed. Once again, alteration can be viewed as reflecting the generic expectations of the audience, as we will see with Joseph Mankiewicz's 1958 adaptation of Greene's *The Quiet American* (1955) or the Boulting brothers' 1947 version of *Brighton Rock*.

A cursory glance at some recent adaptations of works by other writers brings these strategies of adaptation into sharper focus. In the 2001 film of Alan Moore and Eddie Campbell's graphic novel *From Hell* (1999), the main character Frederick Abberline – a middle-aged, portly detective in the original – has morphed into the handsome – and more box-office friendly – figure of Johnny Depp: this is a classic instance of alteration as adaptation. Similarly, there are striking examples of marginalization and expansion in the screen adaptation of Upton Sinclair's novel *Oil!* (1927), *There Will Be Blood* (Paul Thomas Anderson, 2007). The film version plays up the role of the oil prospector Daniel Plainview (played by Daniel Day Lewis) – making him, indeed, somehow emblematic of twentieth-century capitalist America as a whole – and marginalizes the figure of his son, who is in fact the main protagonist in the novel. Peter Jackson's adaptations of J. R. R. Tolkien exemplify the controversies which can surround the implementation of some of these strategies. On the one hand, Jackson's *The Lord of the Rings* (2001–3) film trilogy enjoyed huge commercial and critical success, but received some criticism for what had been omitted or marginalized in the adaptation of Tolkien's half-a-million-word series of novels. On the other, Jackson's next Tolkien enterprise, *The Hobbit* (2012–14), received a lambasting from some quarters for expanding upon and embellishing the basic narrative of Tolkien's comparatively slim 95,000-word novel, to create a three-part film series equal in length (and as it is no doubt anticipated, in critical and commercial success) to *The Lord of the Rings* films.

The success and profile of Jackson's Tolkien adaptations undoubtedly owes a great deal to the tremendous advances in film technology through the years. Things have come a long way since when, during his early years as a film critic, Greene bemoaned the technology of cinema for lacking the evocative power of prose fiction. Advances in editing, computer-generated imagery (CGI), modelling and three-dimensional technology (3D) have facilitated the creation of films with a visual grandeur to match that of Tolkien's fantasy epic. In this regard, adaptive cinema in the early-twenty-first century has been technologically suited to realize the spectacular and fantastical landscapes not only of Tolkien but also of other popular fantasy authors such as C. S. Lewis (whose *Chronicles of Narnia* are the basis of an ongoing series of films [2005—]) and, more recently, J. K. Rowling (whose *Harry Potter* novels were the basis of an enormously lucrative franchise [2001–11]). Through the history of adaptation in cinema, it is interesting to see which writers have appealed and on what terms. As we have seen, writers such as Jane Austen and Charles Dickens, as both canonical and popular authors, continue to have major appeal. In the area of mainstream fiction and film, Ian Fleming's James Bond has had such widespread and lasting appeal that the franchise has run out of original novels to adapt. As with the recent 'reboots' of the Batman and Spider-Man franchises by Christopher Nolan and Sam Raimi (the latter being itself 'rebooted' by the more recent still *The Amazing Spider-Man*), this has led recent adapters of Bond to start again at the beginning, with Daniel Craig starring in the second screen version of Fleming's debut Bond novel, *Casino Royale* (1953), in 2006.

Another practice of the film industry has been to turn to 'living greats' not just as a source but also as potential screenwriters. One of the first notable examples of this trend was Joseph Conrad. The Famous Players-Lasky production company (which eventually became Paramount) paid Conrad $20,000 for the cinematic rights to four of his novels and in 1919 released a film version of Conrad's 1915 novel *Victory*, a major Hollywood release directed by the acclaimed Maurice Tourneur and starring the early screen superstar Lon Chaney. Hollywood later took things a step further by actively courting Conrad to become a screenwriter in his own right. Conrad was paid to develop a film scenario in the early 1920s and, as might be expected, turned to adaptation by transforming one of his own stories, 'Gaspar Ruiz' (1908), into a screenplay – *Gaspar the Strong Man*. Conrad's film career came to nothing: *Gaspar* would remained unfilmed, and he would produce no other screenplays before his death in 1924. Yet the moment remains significant for what it reveals about the early development of the film industry. In a very short space of time, adaptation had quickly become a core component of film-making, with the place of the writer finding increased importance – an importance that would continue to grow with the inauguration of sound cinema as standard practice in the late 1920s onwards, enabling dialogue to become a principle vehicle of narrative on film as in fiction. Following Conrad, cinema would find its own great writers: specialist screenwriters and, more importantly for our purposes, authors who were deftly able to step between novel-writing and screenwriting such as Raymond Chandler, William Faulkner and, of course, Graham Greene.

Although we might think of Greene primarily as a novelist, he was also a prolific writer for the screen. He wrote ten screenplays, eight of which were adaptations (six of which were adaptations of his own works). These include original screenplays for the commercial and propaganda pieces *The Future's in the Air* (1937) and *The New Britain* (1940), adaptations of two plays by John Galsworthy and George Bernard Shaw, *The First and the Last* (*21 Days*, 1940) and *St Joan* (*St Joan*, 1957), as well as adaptations of his own novels and short fiction: *Brighton Rock* (1947), *The Fallen Idol* (1948), *The Third Man* (1949), *Loser Takes All* (1956), *Our Man in Havana* (1959) and *The Comedians* (1967). In addition, he also wrote two works conceived as film 'treatments', *The Tenth Man* (1944) and *No Man's Land* (1950), though these were (unlike that which he wrote in preparation for the screenplay for *The Third Man*) never filmed.

By way of further illuminating some of the prevailing strategies of adaptation, and of laying the ground for the discussion of his works in the following chapters, let us briefly consider Greene's 1978 novel *The Human Factor*. Like his earlier novel *Our Man in Havana* (1958), *The Human Factor* is set during the Cold War. Like that novel, it also centres on a middle-aged, seemingly unremarkable family man named Castle, who is an employee of MI6. Castle has been passing British secrets to the Russians out of gratitude to the communists who helped smuggle his wife Sarah, a black South African, out from under the noses of the Apartheid regime. Castle's section is suspected of the leak and his colleague Davis, thought to be the source, is murdered by his employers. Castle defects to Moscow, promised by his Russian contacts that his wife and adopted son will be following. In a doubly-bitter and – characteristically – deeply cynical ending, Castle learns that this promise will not be kept, and that the secrets he has passed on were of minor importance, used to help establish the credentials of another Russian double agent. Whereas *Our Man in Havana* portrays the British Intelligence community as bungling and incompetent, in *The Human Factor* it is depicted as 'Machiavellian, ruthless' (Watts, 1997, p. 80). Nonetheless, this ruthlessness is still lined with a certain incompetence, as is underlined by the wrongful assassination of Davis, who is more interested in making passes at his secretary than in passing on state secrets. There is also a prevailing sense of inadequacy within this community, which displays a collective nostalgia for an idealized and seemingly less-complicated past – a subtle comment on Britain's post-war imperial decline and diminished importance on a world stage now divided between Soviet Russia and the United States.)

At one level, *The Human Factor* is a re-working of Greene's previous spy fiction, offering a serious take on the same British Intelligence community already lampooned in *Our Man in Havana* (indeed, Greene had conceived of the novel whilst writing *Our Man*). At another, it offers a reworking of his experience within this same community during the Second World War – an experience which also yielded his 1948 novel *The Heart of the Matter*. In this way, the novel can be seen as a piece of self-adaptation, first, of Greene's own biography, and second, of another pre-existing literary work based on that same biographical experience. Many other aspects of Greene's biography are detectable in the novel's finer details: the recreation of Berkhamsted (where Greene grew up), Daintry's flat near St James's Park (based on Greene's own London apartment), Castle's memories of V1 rockets ('buzz bombs' [*Human Factor*, p. 105]) during the Blitz, and Davis's seemingly incongruous love of the poetry of Robert Browning, all draw on Greene's personal background and experiences. The novel is dedicated to his sister Elisabeth, who recruited him to the Secret Intelligence Service in 1941.

In terms of plot, Castle's defection draws heavily on the real-life defection of the British agent Harold 'Kim' Philby in 1963, under whom Greene had worked in SIS (as MI6 was formerly known), and who, like Castle, was also a Russian double agent. One key difference between Castle and Philby, however, is that Castle feels obligated to the Russians rather than convinced by them politically, and this makes his eventual defection both ineluctable and yet avoidable at the same time. Greene had been friends with Philby during his years in SIS and, having written a large part of *The Human Factor*, felt compelled because of this connection to put it aside for some ten years: 'I took the novel up again, telling myself that the Philby affair belonged now sufficiently to the past' (Cited in Tóibín, 2005, p. ix). Intriguingly, Greene had already tackled one aspect of the 'Philby affair' twenty years earlier in *Our Man in Havana*: in that novel the main character Wormold is, like Philby, rewarded with an OBE for his deception (Watts, 1997, p. 65) – a case, as with Wormold's fabrications (his reports to London are wholly fictitious), of life imitating art.

The *Human Factor* quickly became a best-seller, 'enhancing [Greene's] international reputation' (Watts, 1997, p. 80), and, like *Our Man in Havana*, was just as quickly earmarked for adaptation by the Austrian-born director Otto Preminger. Preminger initially approached Greene to adapt the novel for the screen. Greene was, after all, an accomplished writer for the screen as well as of literary fiction, and had by this point already had considerable success adapting not only his own works but also works by other authors, as we have seen – including's Preminger's *St Joan*. Despite this, Greene declined. As it turns out, however, Greene had in a sense already provided the screenplay. As Colm Tóibín observes, *The Human Factor* is 'a book which is as orderly in its structure, at times, as a screenplay' (Tóibín, 2005, p. x).

Accordingly, Tom Stoppard's adaptation of the novel for Preminger's 1979 screen version keeps closely to its source – 'precise almost to Greene's letter and phrase' (Falk, 2000, p. 127) – with only a few notable alterations. As Philip French observed at the time, 'the emblematic [cultural] references to Richardson's *Clarissa* and Ben Nicholson' have been 'changed to *Huckleberry Finn* and Mondrian' (Cited in Falk, 2000, p. 129); these alterations (which French saw as an unnecessary 'dilution' of the novel) were probably made with the film's wider audience in mind – Twain and Mondrian having a more international appeal than their British counterparts Richardson and Nicholson. The screenplay also added a new opening scene. This featured the sinister Doctor Percival foul-hooking a catch while fishing, anticipating his mistakenly 'catching' the wrong man in the sad, love-struck shape of Davis. However, this was perhaps seen as giving a little too much away, and it was later dropped from the film.

Despite the novel's being 'ready-made' for adaptation, that adaptation is on many levels a failure. The cast included contemporary stalwarts of British stage and screen such as Richard Attenborough (as Daintry), Derek Jacobi (as Davis), John Gielgud (as Brigadier Tomlinson), Robert Morley (as Percival) and Nicol Williamson (as Castle), yet arguably some are miscast or give misjudged performances. Equally, Iman's wooden performance as Sarah is, as Neil Sinyard puts it, 'another addition to that gallery of [...] crucial female figures in Greene's film adaptations who are meant to represent the hero's fatal flaw', but 'become instead the film's' (Sinyard, 2003, p. 156). Another reason for the film's failure lies with Preminger. He and Greene had been friends since working together on Preminger's 1957 film of Shaw's *St Joan*. Yet, though an admirer of Preminger's earlier works such as *Carmen Jones* (1954), Greene had serious reservations about the director's more recent output (Falk, 2000, p. 125). The production was also beset by a lack of proper financing, and this impoverishment is clearly evident in the film's sets, in particular its unpersuasive recreation of Moscow (especially when set against Carol Reed's *Our Man in Havana*, shot, evidently at great expense, on location in the Cuban capital). Although this is in keeping with the novel's wilful unglamorousness, and with Greene's original aim to write an antidote to Ian Fleming's Bond novels, this consonance was achieved more by accident than by design.

Another consonance – this time intended – between the book and the film proved to be the latter's undoing. As Quentin Falk glosses: 'One of the many qualities of [the novel] is its relentlessly low-key approach' (Falk, 2000, p. 125). The novel is concerned with the bureaucracy of the Cold War: Castle is 'a first-class administrator' (*HF*, p. 47) who has little in common with the kinds of daring espionage presented by John Buchan or Ian Fleming and more in common with the downbeat 'Smiley' novels of John le Carré (1974–9). However, Preminger's film was unfortunately 'low-key almost to the point of terminal inertia' (Falk, 2000, p. 125). Falk speculates that Preminger 'most likely saw *The Human Factor* as something of a quality comeback' (Falk, 2000, p. 125). Quality was not, however, budgeted for, and Preminger's comeback did not begin, but rather stalled, with *The Human Factor*. Le Carré's Smiley trilogy was the basis of a fondly remembered BBC adaptation in the late 1970s and early 1980s, and it is possible that *The Human Factor* was likewise better suited, in both tone and tenor, to the small screen. As all of this suggests, though many of Greene's works seem immediately suited to adaptation, the adaptive media and methods have not always been suited to the task, and nowhere is this more abundantly clear than in *The Human Factor*.

As a case study, *The Human Factor* raises several issues that will help to define our approach to Greene's works in the chapters which follow. These include fundamental differences in media (in terms of what works on the page in the source text, and what patently does not in its translation to the screen), questions of authorship and originality (in terms of the extent to which Greene or Stoppard or even Preminger can be considered to have 'authored' the film), as well as underlying contexts of history and setting (the novel grew out from the Philby defection and Greene's experience of espionage during the 1940s, whereas the film is firmly a study of the Cold War politics of the late 1970s, when it was made). In addition, *The Human Factor* underlines issues of self-adaptation, appropriation and intertextuality (the novel is both a companion piece to *Our Man in Havana* and an engagement with the genre fiction of Fleming and le Carré), of addition and alteration (in terms of how the screenplay utilizes its original source), as well as freighted questions of fidelity and reception (in terms of the unfavourable critical comparison of the film with the novel, then as now). This issue of reception also reminds us that Greene was not just a novelist and a screenwriter, but also a professional film-reviewer with a lifelong interest in cinema, and that there is a complex interdependence between these artistic activities and interests, as the following chapters will be exploring.

Exercises

- Look at past nominees and winners of film awards (the Oscars, BAFTAs, Golden Globes, and so on), in particular in the categories of 'Best Film' and 'Best Screenplay' (or equivalent). Investigate how many are examples of adaptation as opposed to 'original' works. Consider what this reveals about the cultural status of adaptation; for instance, what does it show us about ideas of 'originality'? In addition, consider to what extent it is possible to create an 'original' adaptation?
- Look at some examples of how film adaptations are marketed with regard to their sources. Do they overtly highlight their literary source or is this relationship more hidden?
- Look at some reviews of film adaptations. Do they mention, fixate on, or ignore the films' source texts? Why do reviewers foreground

the relationship between a film adaptation and its source text in some instances, but not in others? What does this tell us about the relationship between film adaptations and literary texts with regard to their critical reception?

- Choose a work of fiction and a film adaptation of it, and apply the 'Five Creative Strategies of Adaptation'. To this end, you might wish to draw up a table in order to list and compare the examples you find.

Chapter One

Greene in Context

Graham Greene's life spans all ten decades of the twentieth century. He was born into Edwardian Britain in 1904, became a professional author in the late 1920s, and lived an active and creative life until his death in 1991. Greene not only stands as a fascinating product of the twentieth century but also remains one of its most emblematic writers. He was prolific as well as versatile, with an output that covered the broadest variety of genres including novels, short stories, plays, screenplays, reviews, journalism, children's literature, essays, poetry, travel writing, diaries and biographies, not to mention a vast number of letters (a selection of which were published in 2007). Although he will always be regarded, first and foremost, as a novelist, these other achievements should not be considered as examples of mere dabbling: for example, his years as the first film reviewer for the *Spectator* during the 1930s (a position he instigated himself after bemoaning the magazine's neglect of cinema [*Ways of Escape*, p. 58]), and subsequently for *Night and Day* towards the end of that decade, yielded a large and impressive corpus of work which remains to this day a landmark in the craft of film reviewing and a touchstone of modern film criticism.

Cinema occupies an important place in Greene's life and literary career. As David Lodge glosses, 'Greene belonged to the first generation of British writers who grew up with the movies, and his work [...] was deeply influenced by the new medium' (Lodge, 2005, p. vii). It is no accident that Greene's 1971 autobiography, *A Sort of Life*, opens with a description of the New Cinema 'under a green Moorish dome' (p. 11) in Berkhamsted, where he was born and raised. Towards the end of his life he explained the influence of cinema – as distinct from other visual media such as photography – on his prose: 'When I describe a scene, I capture it with the eye of the cine-camera rather than the photographer's eye – which leaves it frozen' (Allain, 1983, p. 132). Greene's early novel *Stamboul Train* (1932) is an interesting case study in this regard. Greene had, in his own words, deliberately 'set out to write a book [...] which with luck might be made into a film' (*WE*, p. 26). Indeed, the sale of *Stamboul Train* to Twentieth Century Fox in May 1933 gave him the first financial security he had had since leaving his editorial post at the *Times* at the end of 1929 in order to commit to writing full-time (Sherry, 1989, p. 475). *Stamboul Train* and the ensuing screen adaptation of it – *Orient Express* (Paul Martin, 1934) – reveal how film and fiction were interdependent for Greene from more or less the beginning of his literary career, inasmuch that film provided the financial stability for Greene to carry on as a writer. Greene also notes that *Stamboul Train* was not only written with its adaptation in mind, but was itself inspired by a film, Edmund Golding's 1932 picture *Grand Hotel* (*WE*, p. 26). As all of this suggests, Greene's professional and artistic relationship with cinema is a complex one, and rarely runs in one direction. From *Stamboul Train* onwards, his fiction has been a popular choice for screen adaptation, with Greene himself often playing a significant role as a screenwriter in the adaptation his own works. Moreover, the appeal of Greene is not limited to cinema: his works have been adapted to the widest range of performance media, including television, radio, theatre and even opera. In this chapter we will be exploring some of the other important contexts that, in addition to cinema, have informed the composition and critical afterlife of his works.

Politics and art

In many ways, it could be argued that Greene's unique status is defined less by his creative diversity than by his paradoxical qualities. These contradictions come into sharp relief when we take a closer look at Greene's politics. Terry Eagleton has argued that Greene was 'a strike breaker during the General Strike' of 1926, and was in later life 'consistently pro-Israel and anti-Arab' (Eagleton, 2007), and Paul Theroux has noted a similar conservatism: 'As a traveller, he greatly preferred nightmare republics to healthy democracies, though as a resident he chose more salubrious places, the isle of Capri, a fashionable district of Paris, and Antibes', to which he moved 'in 1966, as a tax exile' (Theroux, 2005, p. v). Yet Greene cannot be so easily pigeonholed, having leaned as far to the political Left as he did to the Right. He was a member of the Communist Party while at Oxford and, though he later played down this affiliation, traces of it can be found in his later sympathy for communist regimes such as that of Cuba. In fact, he was refused a visa to visit the United States in 1954 because of these same Party affiliations: as Greene mischievously put it in his second memoir *Ways of Escape* (1980), 'The plastic curtain fell [...] and was not lifted again until John Kennedy was President' (*WE*, p. 210). This refusal was also grounded in (and no doubt fed) Greene's staunch anti-Americanism and disdain for US hegemony – whether political, economic or cultural – generally. He was an activist against American involvement in Vietnam in the 1960s and 1970s and supported the Sandinista National Liberation Front (despised and covertly attacked by the US government) in Nicaragua in the 1980s. It comes as little surprise, as Eagleton notes, that Greene was 'a target of FBI surveillance for some 40 years' (Eagleton, 2007). For many critics, Greene's perceived anti-Americanism comes to a head in his 1955 novel *The Quiet American*, an important case study in the adaptation of Greene's works, as we will see. In addition, Greene's complex political background and beliefs may have barred him from entering America, but they did not prevent him working for British Intelligence. He could be both an opponent of the state and a servant of it.

Greene was also contradictory in terms of his art. He was able to span the 'literary' and the 'popular' at a time when these realms were arguably distinct (and even antithetical). Greene himself suggested a qualitative distinction across his own output when he labelled some of his fictions 'novels' and others 'entertainments'. Revealingly, these categories carry with them an added implication when it comes to adaptation: works labelled as 'entertainments' (such as *Stamboul Train* and *Brighton Rock*) were consciously targeted for potential – and potentially lucrative – film deals. As with so much of Greene's art, these categories took shape in dialogue with his cinema-going. In one of his early film reviews he notes: 'Ford Madox Ford has divided fiction into novels and nuvvels. So one may divide films into movie and cinema' (*Night and Day*, 16 December 1937, p. 244): the latter is 'art', while the former is a lesser cultural form but which offers more in the way of entertainment. Accordingly, Michael Stapleton defines Greene's 'entertainments' as works that are 'spare, tough thrillers which present aspects of the human situation in contemporary settings' (Stapleton, 1983, p. 364); meanwhile Neil Sinyard describes them as possessing 'a heady combination of plot, melodrama and suspense, rather than a more overtly serious purpose, be it moral or political' (Sinyard, 2003, p. 99). We can see these distinctions in the generic variation between Greene's debut novel *The Man Within* (1929) – an historical romance about smugglers on the English south coast – or the *joie de vivre* of the globe-trotting *Travels With My Aunt* (1969) – which was, as he later admitted, 'the only book I have written for the fun of it' (*WE*, p. 296) – or the moral complexity and profound characterization of *The Power and the Glory* (1940), the saga of a hunted priest fleeing the persecution of the Catholic church in 1930s Mexico. However, these distinctions between the 'popular' and the 'literary' in Greene's oeuvre were not always entirely clearcut: *Brighton Rock* (1938) was published as 'a novel' in Britain and as 'an entertainment' in the United States (Stapleton, 1983, p. 364). These labels were later dropped for the Collected Edition of Greene's works, published by Heinemann in the 1970s onwards, by which time his literary reputation and popular legacy were assured. Nevertheless, they suggest, like the political and ideological contradictions of his biography, something of the duality of Greene. On the one hand, there is the Greene who shared the same 'contempt for middlebrow tastes' that was a 'national sport' amongst contemporary writers as diverse as J. B. Priestley and Virginia Woolf, as Lawrence Napper has argued (Napper, 2000, p. 117). On the other, there is the Greene whose achievement rests, in part, in having created abidingly popular 'entertainments'.

Greene's achievement and legacy rests not just in his works, but also through the adaptation of his works. For instance, in writing the novella of *The Third Man* (1950) exclusively as a film treatment prior to writing the screenplay, Greene created the character of Harry Lime, an extraordinary villain of the modern age who immediately became an icon of contemporary popular culture. The film of *The Third Man* (Carol Reed, 1949) continues to be one of the most highly regarded examples of British cinema and, half a century after its release, topped the British Film Institute's 1999 poll of the hundred 'greatest' British films of the twentieth century. Beyond this, the success of the film of *The Third Man* led to spin-offs such as the BBC's *The Third Man: The Adventures of Harry Lime* (1951–2), a series of 52 radio plays featuring Orson Welles recreating his legendary screen role, and BBC television's *The Third Man* (1959–65), with Michael Rennie in the title role. Although Greene was not involved in the script work for either series (having shrewdly sold the rights for a substantial sum), they stand as fascinating examples of the power of Greene's artistic imagination: to create a character who could continue to live beyond its creator's original vision, come alive in the performance media and enter the popular cultural imagination.

Catholicism and 'Greeneland'

Another of the paradoxes surrounding Greene concerns his religious beliefs and the presence of these beliefs in his works. Greene converted to Catholicism as a young man and though he would later mischievously refer to himself as a 'Catholic agnostic' (*Observer*, 12 March 1978, p. 35), issues of faith, sin and guilt are recurrent themes, if not preoccupations, in his novels. Although Greene's Catholicism is a compelling aspect of his biographical and creative identity, he grew increasingly disgruntled by what he felt was a critical obsession with it. He bridled at being called a 'Catholic writer' – a 'detestable term!' – preferring instead to be known as 'a writer who happens to be Catholic' (*WE*, p. 74). Yet Greene never concealed his Catholic identity, and this is reflected in his reception: *The End of the Affair* (1951), Greene's morally ambiguous and most explicit study of adultery, was awarded the 1952 Catholic Literary Award, while the equally controversial *The Power and the Glory* won the approval of Pope Paul VI (*WE*, p. 87). According to David Pryce-Jones, Greene's unorthodox and, at times, wavering Catholicism is undoubtedly one reason he attained such an international profile (Pryce-Jones, 1973, p. 1). As Eagleton puts it: 'Greene was, in short, that most honorific of Catholics, a lapsed or unorthodox one', 'well aware that the prodigal son has a higher status than the loyal stay-at-home' (Eagleton, 2007).

At the same time, Greene's Catholicism arguably won him as many enemies as friends. It certainly prevented him winning other awards, most notably the Nobel Prize for Literature during the 1950s. According to Norman Sherry, Greene was a clear contender for the accolade, but the Swedish writer Arthur Lundkvist, who held great influence as a member of the Swedish Academy in charge of selecting the laureates, was instrumental in Greene not getting the award (Sherry, 1994, p. 452). Lundkvist's most public condemnation of Greene is to be found in his review of Greene's stage play *The Living Room*, which he denounced as Catholic 'propaganda of the most vulgar type' (Cited in Sherry, 2004, p. 721) for its perceived attack on Sigmund Freud and the modern science of psychology. This is, if anything, ironic: Greene was a convert to the value of psychoanalysis (at 17) some time before he became a convert to Catholicism (at 22), and throughout his career lauded the power of the unconscious in the process of literary creation.

Greene's idiosyncratic brand of Catholicism also occasioned an unfavourable response to his works among his contemporaries, as is typified by a notorious review of his 1948 novel *The Heart of the Matter* by George Orwell (Orwell, 1973), which damned not only that novel, but Greene's works as a whole, for suggesting that the believing sinner can be saint-like. The paradoxical concept of the 'sanctified sinner' (as the title of Orwell's review had it) is acutely evident in *The Power and the Glory*, the nameless protagonist of which – the 'whisky priest' – is a self-destructive alcoholic, caught up in the anti-Catholic purges in 1930s Mexico (about which Greene had reported in his 1939 travelogue *The Lawless Roads*). The priest is running for his life from the new regime and yet continues to perform his religious duties, albeit in a spirit of reluctance, and by the end of the novel, and despite his overriding sense of inadequacy, weakness and personal sin, he attains a redemptive and transcendent holiness. The novel was later adapted for the screen as *The Fugitive* (John Ford, 1947), starring Henry Fonda in the title role. The change in title is noteworthy, suggesting more of an adventure or 'pursuit' thriller (as in the highly popular 1960s US television series of the same name), in place of the allusion to the Lord's Prayer of the original, and seemingly closer in spirit to Greene's early 'entertainments'. However, though the film received some positive high-profile reviews, and though Ford himself felt it was his greatest work to date, it was a commercial flop, and Ford was adjudged to have slipped into self-indulgence and to have produced a film of heavy-handed 'religious symbolism' (Davis, 1997, p. 198). What made the novel exceptional, not only among Greene's literary works but also among contemporary literature as a whole, did not necessarily translate well to the screen. There are other important 'sinners-as-saints' in Greene's fiction, such as Sarah Miles, the adulterous and yet virtuous figure in *The End of the Affair*. More problematically still, there are Catholic characters such as Pinkie Brown in *Brighton Rock*, who are irremediably 'evil' and yet somehow deserving of the reader's sympathy and even religious salvation. These two novels are the sources of several notable film adaptations of Greene's works, as we will explore.

John Spurling compels us to view the religious aspect of Greene's fiction as something much more complex than the religious credo of some of his characters:

> Greene does explore real pain and unhappiness and not always solely in his protagonists. The pain is felt through his protagonists, but it is often drawn off the subsidiary characters, the protagonists acting as a kind of conduit for whatever angst or suffering is around, much in the way that a priest does or is supposed to do. In this sense, one can say that Greene's fiction has a genuine religious dimension, not to be confused with that melodramatic backdrop of good or evil which he used as a way of raising the stakes and laying on the colours. (Spurling, 1983, pp. 72–3)

At the same time, and despite the massive amount of criticism devoted to his devotion, we should perhaps not become overly obsessed with Greene's Catholicism as the key to unlocking meaning in his works. As J. P. Kulshrestha argues, Greene was 'obsessed with good and evil as human problems, not Catholic problems' (Kulshrestha, 1977, p. 228).

If the 'sanctified sinner' is characteristic of Greene, so, too, is the concept of 'Greeneland' – a seedy, melancholic, frequently exotic landscape, wherein profoundly flawed (frequently Catholic) individuals struggle against a context of adversity, cynicism, and claustrophobia, occasionally attaining through this ordeal a degree of personal redemption. As Norman Sherry explains, the term was 'first coined by Arthur Calder Marshall in 1940' and has been 'overused by critics' ever since (Sherry, 1994, p. 217), and, like other distinctive literary terms such as 'Conradian' or 'Kafkaesque', it has even been included in the *Oxford English Dictionary*. As with his opposition to being labelled a 'Catholic writer', Greene bridled at the term: '"This is Indo-China", I want to exclaim, "this is Mexico, this is Sierra Leone carefully and accurately described"' (*WE*, p. 77). Greene hereby defends the representational fidelity and objectivity of his fictional works, which a metaphysical term such as 'Greeneland' would seem to deny. At the same time, Greene undermines this by claiming 'not [to be] interested in landscape, or how a house may be decorated', 'except in so far as these things affect the evolution of any of the characters in the novel' (Cited in Duràn, 1994, pp. 14–15). Although attempting to condense key themes and motifs of Greene's oeuvre into one word is inadequate, 'Greeneland' remains a useful critical term, albeit one that should be approached with caution.

In the same way, biographical approaches can sometimes be misleading, not least in the case of Greene who can be playful and even disingenuous in his self-presentation, which often borders on the self-mythologizing. Nevertheless, Greene's life-as-text can map onto his writing, and the adaptation of his writing, in rewarding ways. If his unhappy school life, his failed (and equally unhappy) marriage and numerous affairs and his Catholicism may not have determined his writing, they undeniably leave an indelible imprint on it. The same can be said of Greene's extensive travels and experience of political turmoil and conflict. Greene was not a writer of the cork-lined study, but a restless and inveterate traveller, and this feeds into the tropes and terrains of 'Greeneland.' He visited troubled parts of the world during times of political and religious oppression, revolution and war. His regular journeys through the years included dangerous visits to a politically tumultuous South and Central America, Vietnam at the height of the French war, Cuba during the communist revolution, Malaya during the Emergency, Haiti during the Papa Doc era, the Congo during the violent collapse of Belgian rule, Kenya during the Mau Mau Uprising and Northern Ireland during the peak of the Troubles. Greene's experiences of the Blitz in London during the Second World War – which gave fictional shape to both *The Ministry of Fear* (1943) and *The End of the Affair* – were similarly intense, as were his years as a spy in Sierra Leone later in the war, which he subsequently revisited in *The Heart of the Matter*, *Our Man in Havana* (1958) and *The Human Factor* (1978). With Greene there is a degree of adventure-seeking or even self-destructiveness, which dates back to his reputed fascination with games of Russian roulette as a teen (revisited in *A Sort of Life* [p. 92]), and which comes to a head during the 1950s. As Neil Sinyard observes, Greene's depression was at its worst during this period and this – combined with his visits to some of the world's most dangerous places – led some friends to believe he was 'unlikely to survive the decade' (Sinyard, 2003, p. 5). Not for nothing did Greene choose as his 'epigraph' some lines from Robert Browning: 'Our interest's on the dangerous edge of things [...] The giddy line midway' (*A Sort of Life*, p. 85).

Greene and other authors

Greene's suggestive borrowing from Browning brings us to the issue of influence. Although Greene has a distinctive and versatile authorial style – as the critical shorthand 'Greeneland' confirms – he was also much influenced by his literary predecessors. No writer emerges from a vacuum, but few were more open about their influences than Greene. Given Greene's literary standing and reputation, some of these early influences and inspirations are perhaps surprising. To modern readers, Marjorie Bowen's *The Viper of Milan* (1904) is a lengthy and full-blooded historical melodrama, but Greene is unequivocal in determining its impact on him as a teen after an 'omnivorous childhood' of reading (*ASL*, p. 116): 'From that moment I began to write. All other possible futures slid away' (*Collected Essays*, p. 16).

Other influences on Greene during his early years include the popular adventure stories and colonial romances of nineteenth-century authors such as R. M. Ballantyne (Greene's first 'real book' [*CE*, p. 14] was *The Coral Island* [1858]), H. Rider Haggard and Robert Louis Stevenson (the latter perhaps unsurprisingly: Greene's mother was Stevenson's first cousin). Greene also found a particular appeal in the adventure stories and spy fiction of the Scottish novelist John Buchan. As he later extolled: 'John Buchan was the first to realize the enormous dramatic value of adventure in familiar surroundings happening to unadventurous men' (*CE*, p. 167). Buchan's influence can also be detected during Greene's early Continental travels, such as his early visit to Germany, during which Greene imagined himself participating in 'a thriller [...] rather in Buchan's manner' (*ASL*, p. 102).

Buchan wrote many thrillers that enjoyed huge popularity and had an incalculable influence on the 'thriller' genre as a whole, and across different media. His most celebrated novel, *The Thirty-Nine Steps* (1915), was to become a popular source for film adaptations by Alfred Hitchcock (1935), Ralph Thomas (1959) and Don Sharp (1978), as well as numerous television, radio and theatre versions. Many of these adaptations work extremely well, not least because Buchan created a paradigmatic plot that would become a favourite of the popular film industry. The innocent 'man-on-the-run' plot will recur in films such as *The Clouded Yellow* (Ralph Thomas, 1951), *North by Northwest* (Alfred Hitchcock, 1959), or the television series *The Fugitive* (Quinn Martin Productions, 1963–7).

Buchan's novel centres on a Scottish adventurer and Boer War veteran called Richard Hannay (a recurring hero of Buchan's). Hannay is running for his life, partly because some of his acquaintances have been murdered, but also because he knows that he will be the chief police suspect. Time and again, Hannay narrowly escapes death or capture. As his desperate adventure continues, he becomes increasingly embroiled in intrigue and conspiracy and gradually discovers that Britain is in danger from a German plot; revealingly, Greene's most successful thriller *The Ministry of Fear* (1943) likewise features just such a plot; just as revealingly, many of his early works are driven by, or feature, a similar Buchan-esque 'man-on-the-run' plot, including *The Man Within* (1929), *Stamboul Train* (1932), *A Gun for Sale* (1936), *Brighton Rock* (1938), *The Confidential Agent* (1939) and *The Power and the Glory* (1940).

In fact, the same can be said of Greene's later fiction. The enormous dramatic value of the Buchan-esque plot proves to be a frequent point of reference where characters who are unadventurous by nature – from Scobie in *The Heart of the Matter* (1948) and Martins in *The Third Man* (1950), to Wormold in *Our Man in Havana* (1958) and Charles Fortnum in *The Honorary Consul* (1973) – find themselves caught up in life-and-death situations. Where Greene departs from Buchan is in his treatment of the familiar and the exotic: the well-travelled Greene relishes in evoking locations that are unfamiliar to his readers, whether it is Mexico during the religious purges of the late 1930s (*The Power and the Glory*), post-war Austria of the late 1940s (*The Third Man*) or the pre-revolutionary Cuba of the late 1950s (*Our Man in Havana*). Meanwhile in the case of *Brighton Rock*, the popular seaside town of the title is *defamiliarized* and displaced by a world of spiritual angst and mortal danger, becoming in the process another of Greene's 'dangerous edges', every bit as hazardous for its protagonists as, for instance, the violence of 1960s Haiti (*The Comedians*) or 1970s Argentina (*The Honorary Consul*).

Buchan's works are significant not just in terms of their popular influence, but also in terms of their political foresight. A case in point is the neglected novel *The Power-House* (1916), Buchan's thriller about an anarchist plot to destroy Western civilization. As in *The Thirty-Nine Steps*, the conspiracy is thwarted through a series of exciting close-shaves and the derring-do of Edward Leithen, another recurrent hero of Buchan's. The novel articulates some eerily prophetic aspects, given the era of its production. One character is a German professor who shares his vision of the future with Leithen: 'Some day there will come the marriage of knowledge and will, and then the world will march' (*Power-House*, p. 77). It is a vision of the military totalitarianism that would come to haunt the twentieth century, an all-consuming 'iconoclasm, the swallowing of formulas' (*PH*, p. 81). In *The Power-House*, Western civilization as a whole is shown as being at risk. As another character puts it: 'You think that a wall as solid as the earth separates civilization from barbarism. I tell you the division is a thread, a sheet of glass' (*PH*, pp. 64–5). Although not a 'political' novel as such, Buchan's depiction of jostling ideologies in *The Power-House* is not far from Greene's *The Third Man* or the similarly prophetic works *The Quiet American* or *Our Man in Havana*, which present individuals caught up in the tectonic shifts of international politics and global conflict.

Another key influence on Greene was the Polish-born novelist Joseph Conrad. There are strong parallels to be drawn between their respective lives and works: both had traumatic upbringings (Conrad was raised in political exile and lived in France before settling in England); both were ambivalent in their political and religious views; both drew for their fiction upon an extensive experience of travel (Conrad had served in the French and British merchant marines before becoming a writer); and both combined a methodical and frequently perfectionist approach to their literary craft with an eye for generic experimentation. If Buchan was very much (to borrow Greene's terminology) a writer of popular 'entertainments' rather than more literary (and by implication less popular) 'novels', Conrad was, like Greene, an able exponent of both 'high' and 'low'. Indeed, Conrad's own influences, like Greene's, offer a revealing mixture of high and low: he was as much an admirer of the sea tales of Captain Frederick Marryat as the novels of Gustave Flaubert. Whereas Greene grew up with the cinema, Conrad came to writing literary fiction during a similarly significant shift in the visual and literary arts, with the emergence of Impressionism and literary Modernism giving rise to works such as *Heart of Darkness* (1899) – Conrad's celebrated and controversial exposé of the horrors and human cost of European colonialism in Africa, in which the presumed bulwark of Western civilization is shown to be an insubstantial veneer. Conrad's output was, like Greene's, generically broad and varied, encompassing light historical romances (such as *Romance* [1903], co-written with Ford Madox Ford), colonial and adventure fiction (such as *Lord Jim* [1900]), serious political works (including his masterpiece *Nostromo* [1904]), essays, journalism (he was briefly a contributor to the *Daily Mail*) and even propaganda during the First World War ('The Unlighted Coast' [1916]). A decade before Buchan's *The Power-House*, Conrad wrote *The Secret Agent* (1907), his darkly comic exploration of political anarchism and domestic upheaval in turn-of-the-century London which arguably invented the modern spy novel (Moore, 1996, p. 234).

Greene condemned his early attempts at writing fiction as 'bastard Conradese tortuosity' (Cited in Sherry, 1989, p. 411). The phrase recalls Conrad's self-description – and denunciation – of his early magazine fiction as 'secondhand Conradese' (Karl and Davies, 1983, p. 302): Greene's early statement of authorial self-fashioning, in other words, ironically apes Conrad's own. There is a potent and revealing description of Conrad's 'haunting' effect on Greene's early fiction in his 1971 memoir *A Sort of Life*. Greene describes the realization upon the completion of his second novel, *The Name of Action* (1930), that he had absented himself as author altogether: 'all that was left in the heavy pages [...] was the distorted ghost of Conrad' (*ASL*, p. 147). Greene wryly notes that typically the apprentice writer mines his or her own biography for material; yet with his own fledgling attempts, he had 'gone too far in the opposite direction' (*ASL*, p. 147), and it was partly for this reason that he would later suppress the republication of *The Name of Action*, along with its successor *Rumour at Nightfall* (1931).

Just as Greene detected Conrad's influence, so, too, did reviewers of his early fiction, who frequently remarked upon the consonances between the two authors. Typifying this, one early reviewer described Greene's characters as 'hav[ing] stepped from the pages of Conrad' (*New Statesman*, 8 November 1930, p. 148), while another uncertainly posited Greene himself as being 'somewhere between Stevenson and Conrad' (*Nation and Athenæum*, 3 August 1929, p. 602) – an aptly liminal state, given the characteristic fascination with 'in-betweenness' in his works, be it the wavering between political or religious commitment (Fowler in *The Quiet American*; Sarah in *The End of the Affair*), or the gap between youth and adulthood, and with it, innocence and corruption (Philip in 'The Basement Room' [1935]): these collectively comprise that 'dangerous edge of things' which Greene, borrowing not from Conrad but from Browning, offered as an epigraph for his works as a whole.

Conrad's influence on Greene is perhaps most readily detectable in that part of 'Greeneland' concerned with the colonial (and soon-to-be ex-colonial) or developing worlds, from the Vietnam of *The Quiet American* (1955) to the Haiti of *The Comedians* (1966). As John Spurling puts it: 'No European writer since Conrad has put the hot, poor and foully governed places of the earth on paper as vividly as Greene' (Spurling, 1983, p. 74). Greene's debt to Conrad can also be felt in his political and spy novels. Greene had a particularly strong admiration for *The Secret Agent* (R. Greene, 2007, pp. 163–4) and its influence is pervasive, not least in Greene's fifth novel *It's a Battlefield* (1934). Like Conrad's novel, it features a murky

London setting and an equally murky political situation with which an Assistant Commissioner, formerly of the colonial police, is trying to get to grips, much like his Conradian counterpart. Meanwhile in his late novel *The Human Factor* (1978), one of the main protagonist's spy contacts is a pornographer, recalling the use of a similar front in *The Secret Agent* – a novel also alluded to when the same protagonist, feeling the burden of his duplicity, is compared to 'an anarchist, carrying a time bomb' (*Human Factor*, p. 135) – recalling Conrad's disturbing creation the Professor, arguably the first representation of the suicide bomber in Western literature. Another contact is, like Conrad, a Pole, and like Conrad's son, called Boris. And of course the novel's epigraph, crystallizing the problematic ties made by its hero, is adapted from *Victory*: 'he who forms a tie is lost. The germ of corruption has entered into his soul.'

According to Robert Pendleton, these words not only underscore the dangers of commitment which prove the main character's undoing (the 'human factor' of the title); more important, they also capture something of Greene's own problematic ties with Conrad: 'This "germ of corruption" may stand as a metaphor for Greene and Conrad's intertextuality as well as for their common themes of faith and betrayal.' Similarly, 'the germ of corruption' 'takes root in Greene's early fiction' in the form of 'a complex affinity between two writers engaged in similar generic and thematic endeavours' (Pendleton, 1996, pp. 158–9). The metaphor is also richly suggestive of a contagion the effects of which are not easily cured, and it was not for nothing that Greene would elsewhere refer to Conrad's 'disastrous influence' (Cited in Pendleton, 1996, p. 159).

This 'germ of corruption' had such a detrimental effect on Greene's early fiction that he claims to have refrained from reading Conrad in a bid to attenuate, if not excise, his influence. In particular, *Heart of Darkness* seems to have left a deep, even damaging, impression on Greene: 'It makes one despair of the book I am finishing, of any book I am now likely to write, but at the same time filled me with longing to write finely' (Cited in Sherry, 1989, p. 421). Greene makes the almost ecclesiastical insistence that this 'vow' of not reading Conrad was 'kept for more than a quarter of a century', when in 1959 he found himself journeying up the Congo, a copy of *Heart of Darkness* in hand, to gather material for his new novel *A Burnt-Out Case* (1961) – by which time his own authorial persona, shaped over the course of some sixteen novels, was comparatively secure. Featuring a journey up the River Congo, and the corresponding 'inner journey' of its main protagonist,

A Burnt-Out Case best sums up the intertextuality between Greene and Conrad, and is the novel in which the abiding 'anxiety of influence' is most openly confronted. According to his biographer Norman Sherry, Greene felt that this 'would be his last novel'; that he was, like the architect 'who has lost his vocation' at the heart of the novel, creatively speaking 'a burnt-out case'. As Sherry speculates, Greene could not have been unaware that there was a neat symmetry to the fact that, having as a young writer worried about Conrad's influence, and the influence of *Heart of Darkness* in particular, he should 'try his hand at setting a novel' – perhaps his last – 'in Conrad territory' (Sherry, 2004, p. 258).

Interestingly, this intertextuality between the two authors is echoed in the way their fiction was popular – and well suited – for adaptation, becoming re-written, re-worked and re-deployed in various new and different contexts. Like Greene, Conrad's locations and moral landscapes have proved rich, if often problematic, manna for the film industry. *Victory* (1915) was the first of Conrad's novels to be filmed (Maurice Tourneur, 1919) and has been frequently adapted since; *The Secret Agent* (1907) was filmed as *Sabotage* (Alfred Hitchcock, 1936); 'The Duel' (1908) became *The Duellists* (Ridley Scott, 1977) and, most famously, *Heart of Darkness* (1899) was the key source (albeit uncredited at the time) for *Apocalypse Now* (Francis Ford Coppola, 1979). Other recent adaptations of Conrad's works include *Hanyut* (U-Wei Haji Saari, 2011), based on his debut novel *Almayer's Folly* (1895), and *The Secret Sharer* (Peter Fudakowski, 2013), from his 1909 short story of the same name.

Conrad is today seen as a literary giant, both in terms of his contribution to Modernism and his influence on authors since. Yet this perhaps overshadows his engagement with and adaptation of popular forms to 'higher' cultural ends – most famously his engagement with contemporary adventure fiction and the imperial gothic in *Heart of Darkness*. At the same time, Conrad did not see himself as 'a writer for a limited coterie' (Author's Note, *Chance*, p. viii), and continuously strived to reach popular audiences, finally achieving this with *Chance* (1914) – a novel which was aimed as much at women readers as his earlier sea stories and adventure fiction were at male audiences. In addition, Conrad was, like Greene after him, an adapter of his own works, and this again sees him engage with popular culture. These self-adaptations include two stage dramatizations of his fiction (*The Secret Agent* and *Laughing Anne*) and a screenplay based upon his short story 'Gaspar Ruiz' (1908), written shortly before his death in 1924. Although these were unsuccessful (only one of the scripts, his stage adaptation of *The Secret Agent*, was produced and closed after only a few days) – they demonstrate an enterprising spirit on Conrad's part, and gesture to another link with Greene. As John Spurling has argued: 'One of the most admirable and characteristic things about Greene is the way that he has constantly sought to escape from the straitjacket of his own success', 'by expanding his repertoire, both with new modes of fiction and with excursions into other forms of writing' (Spurling, 1983, p. 53). Yet we should not overlook that from the very beginning of his literary career, and long before his critical reputation was assured, Greene was already making these excursions. He experimented with poetry, the short story form and travel writing, and arguably the most significant of these literary endeavours in terms of its impact on his fiction is his experience as a film reviewer.

Exercises

• Look closely at a novel by Buchan or Conrad or a film adaptation of their work. Consider the ways in which issues of popular genre (such as the thriller, adventure fiction and so on) are mediated. In addition, consider the ways in which characterization and location are established.

• Consider intertextuality as adaptation by comparing one of Conrad's works with one of Greene's (for instance, *Heart of Darkness* with *A Burnt-Out Case*). What elements of the former can you identity in the latter – in terms of plot, theme, narrative structure or style?

Greene the film reviewer

Greene's earliest writings on cinema were for the *Oxford Outlook* in 1925 while still an undergraduate, during which time he was a keen reader of film criticism as well a practitioner – in particular of the magazine *Close Up*, to which the influential Russian director, film theorist (and contemporary of Sergei Eisenstein), Vsevolod Pudovkin, 'contributed articles on montage' (*WE*, p. 58). Greene would also write several film-related pieces for the *Times* in the late 1920s, further honing his craft. However, his career as a reviewer began in earnest in 1935 when he was appointed film critic for the

Spectator – a role in which he would continue until 1940. As he recalls in *Ways of Escape* (1980): 'I was talking to Derek Verschoyle, the Literary Editor of the *Spectator*. The *Spectator* had hitherto neglected films and I suggested to him I should fill the gap – I thought in the unlikely event of his accepting it might be fun for two or three weeks. I never imagined it would remain fun for four and a half years' (*WE*, p. 58). Greene's career as a film reviewer may have been short, but it gave the young writer invaluable training in the language of film, and this would become instrumental to Greene's direct involvement in cinema over coming decades and vital to his development as a writer of literary fiction. For critics such as David Pryce-Jones, it is Greene's screenwriting experience, rather than his experience as a film reviewer, that had a direct impact on his fiction: 'plainly his style and construction owes something to the effects of cutting and dissolving from shot to shot, learnt in this capacity' (Pryce-Jones, 1973, p. 71). Greene himself, however, would disagree: 'I don't think my style as a writer has been influenced by my work for the cinema. My style has been influenced by my *going to the cinema*' (Cited in Donaghy, 1992, p. 75; emphasis added).

Greene's assertion reveals how his role as a critic helped tutor his creative endeavour. For example, he believed that 'the cinema had certain advantages for a writer. In special circumstances it produced the right mood to do creative work' (Cited in Sherry, 1989, p. 244). Peter Mudford adds that in writing over four hundred film reviews Greene was compelled 'to crystallize his own attitudes, to develop in the broadest sense an aesthetic' (Mudford, 1996, p. 19). The impact of Greene's cinema-going on his literary craft was also partly economic: he 'was still not earning enough [writing] books to make a living', and it was partly thanks to his work as a reviewer for the *Spectator* that he 'could make ends meet' (*WE*, p. 75). As with the earlier sale of *Stamboul Train* in 1934, writing on film enabled him to remain, and become a better, writer of fiction.

The period that saw Greene's emergence as a professional film reviewer was also a fascinating era for cinema. During his time as a film critic for the *Oxford Outlook* during the 1920s, silent cinema was the norm; yet when he became a reviewer for the *Spectator* a decade later, sound had become well established and other technological advances – notably colourization – were becoming more widespread. Greene engages with popular genres from comedy to horror and we find him expressing a preference for films with mass appeal – 'the Westerns, the crime films, the farces, the frankly commercial' – over more 'respectable' but staid genres such as the 'biopic' (*WE*, p. 60). In addition, Greene also reviews (to use the terms outlined earlier) 'cinema' as well as 'movies' – that which would now be regarded as 'art' cinema. As Henry J. Donaghy observes, Greene's reviews are notable for 'their [...] passionate wishes for better cinema' (Donaghy, 1992, p. 148). In an interesting reflection of the variety of films on offer in British cinemas during the 1930s, Greene does not limit himself to those produced in Britain or by Hollywood. His reviews frequently consider French, German and Soviet films, and he provides a valuable perspective on these examples of national cinemas. Wherever they are from, and to whichever audiences they appeal, many of the films Greene reviews are adaptations. He typically draws attention to the source texts and reveals the depth of his literary knowledge and strength of his opinion, and this in turn suggests the extent to which his later experience as a screenwriter learned much from his years as a reviewer.

Greene's career as a film critic took him as far as the outbreak of the Second World War and accordingly reflect the cinemas of propaganda and escapism. For example, in a twinned review of *The Light That Failed* (William Wellman, 1939) – adapted from Rudyard Kipling's 1890 novel – and *The Old Maid* (Edmund Goulding, 1939) – based on Edith Wharton's 1924 short novel – Greene praises both films for their ability 'to jerk the waiting tear out of its duct', and suggests both will have 'every tenth man and woman weeping in the dark'. Greene cannot help but remark how 'in a world of bombed towns tears will fall with delirious ease over' an 'improbable' tale like *The Old Maid* (*Spectator*, 19 January 1940, pp. 364–5). The impact of the war can also be felt in the structure of his reviews, as well as in their subject matter. In *Ways of Escape* he recalls beginning to write a review of the Henry Fonda vehicle *Young Mr Lincoln* (John Ford, 1939): 'If there is something a little absentminded about that review, it is because, just as I began to write it on the morning of September 3, 1939, the first air-raid siren of the war sounded and I laid the review aside so as to make notes from my high Hampstead lodging on the destruction of London below. [...] Then the all-clear sounded and I returned to Henry Fonda' (*WE*, p. 58).

Greene could celebrate major individual talents in cinema such as Charlie Chaplin and in his review of *Modern Times* (Charles Chaplin, 1936) he praised what he evidently regarded as the sheer brilliance of Chaplin's comic inventiveness, while equating him – in an unusual juxtaposition – with Conrad for his exploration of 'courage, loyalty, labour', 'against the same nihilistic background of purposeless suffering' (*Spectator*, 14 February 1936, pp. 73–5). Greene also celebrated individual actors, such as in the unambiguously titled review 'The Genius of Peter Lorre'. He sees Lorre as a unique and exceptionally talented performer despite – in a fascinating contention – having not 'appeared in a good film since *M*' (*World Film News*, July 1936, pp. 403–4). At the same time, Greene was never scared to attack established filmmakers whose work in his opinion was overrated, and in so doing challenge the established critical orthodoxy. One memorable target was Alfred Hitchcock. In 'The Genius of Peter Lorre', Greene plays up the actor's success even when 'trapped' within 'Hitchcock's deplorable *Secret Agent*' (*World Film News*, July 1936, p. 404). Greene also produced a detailed and derogatory review of Hitchcock's *Secret Agent*, an adaptation of the W. Somerset Maugham novel *Ashenden* (1928). He damns Hitchcock with the faint praise that he is 'a clever director' (*Spectator*, 15 May 1936, p. 102), and laments that Hitchcock is allowed to produce and write his own films, given that 'as a producer he has no sense of continuity and as a writer he has no sense of life'. All the film deserves is 'laughter' at 'Mr Hitchcock's inadequate sense of reality' (p. 102). In addition, he feels Hitchcock has ruined Maugham's *Ashenden* because in his adaptation 'nothing is left of that witty and realistic fiction' (p. 102). Greene's enmity for Hitchcock lingered. During the late 1950s, when the director's star was even higher thanks partly to the endeavours of the highly influential *Cahiers du Cinéma* school of criticism, Greene refused Hitchcock the film rights to *Our Man in Havana*, preferring to see the film made by Carol Reed ('I still believe I was right', 'whatever Monsieur Truffaut may say' [*WE*, p. 59]). Yet despite Greene's hostility towards Hitchcock, there are compelling parallels to be drawn between the two. Neil Sinyard follows Raymond Durgnat (1974) in arguing that both Greene and Hitchcock consistently display 'the perceptual sophistication of stream-of-consciousness whilst retaining the significant specificity of plot and place' (Sinyard, 2003, p. 107). Sinyard even goes so far as to describe these apparently antagonistic artists to be in fact 'the most fascinating complimentary couple of literature and film' (Sinyard, 2003, p. 108).

In our own time, *The Bride of Frankenstein* (James Whale, 1935) is generally regarded as a masterpiece of the Universal horror films and exceptional for its early demonstration that sequels could be effective and successful (it was a sequel to *Frankenstein* [James Whale, 1931]). It is also a pioneering example in the genre of the screen adaptation of fiction, for beginning with a framing 'biopic' in the form of a prologue featuring the novel's author Mary Shelley, played by Elsa Lanchester, who also takes the role of the eponymous monster/ bride. Although Greene commends the 'strange electric beauty of Miss Elsa Lanchester as Frankenstein's second monster', his overall opinion suggests that this adaptation is part of a franchise which has not merely done a cruel disservice to Shelley's original vision, but that the torment has only just begun:

> Poor harmless Mary Shelley, when she dreamed that she was watched by pale, yellow, speculative eyes between the curtains of her bed, set in motion a vast machinery of actors, of sound systems and trick shots and yes-men. It rolls on indefinitely, the first dream and the first elaboration of it in her novel, *Frankenstein*, gathering silliness and solemnity as it goes; presently, I have no doubt, it will be colour-shot and televised; later in the Brave New World to become a smelly. But the one genuine moment of horror, when Mrs Shelley saw the yellow eyes, vanished long ago; and there is nothing in *The Bride of Frankenstein* at the Tivoli to scare a child. (*Spectator*, 5 July 1935, p. 5)

For Greene, this now much-celebrated sequel is nothing more than 'the dream of a committee of film executives' who have created a 'pompous, badly acted film, full of absurd anachronisms and inconsistencies' (p. 6). For many in film and adaptation studies, however, *The Bride of Frankenstein* has aged well and, although it does not 'scare' (if it ever did), it remains an atmospheric and, frequently, a sharp and witty horror movie. Greene's review is noteworthy not just for its challenge to critical and popular opinion. Here, as elsewhere, Greene's ire is directed less at the film itself than at the cynical nature of the Hollywood film industry, and this was especially true of his opinion of adaptations of literary works. The 'horror' of this particular film lies not in the content but in the way that content has been adapted for the screen. In this way, Greene's film criticism offers a 'wide view' that stretches beyond the close aesthetic analysis of the works he was reviewing to embrace the contexts behind them.

If Greene could condemn the film industry, he was even more critical of film censorship. Barely a month after reviewing *The Bride of Frankenstein*, Greene used his review of another horror picture, *The Hands of Orlac* (Karl Freund, 1935), as a forum to attack the British Board of Film Censors (BBFC), which had tried to ban the film. He denounced the Board as an organization comprised of 'retired Army officers and elderly ladies of no occupation' (*Spectator*, 9 August

1935, p. 16). For Greene, the film is well directed by Freund and it would be 'a thousand pities' if censorship prevented audiences from seeing Peter Lorre's much-praised performance in the lead role of Doctor Gogol. Yet again, the film is an adaptation, here based on Maurice Renard's 1920 novel *Les Mains d'Orlac*, and Greene extends his review to consider the fiction behind it. He avoids the specific issue of adaptation, however, and instead extrapolates the decisions of the BBFC in relation to fiction more broadly. Provocatively, Greene argues that it may be 'sexual perversity' that makes us read Henry James's *The Turn of the Screw* (1898) when 'all the house is abed', but demands to know why 'our pet vice be denied all satisfaction' (p. 16). Greene also campaigned against literary censorship, and was vocal in his support of Vladimir Nabokov's *Lolita* (1959), about the illicit love of an older man for an underage girl, and, before this, Radclyffe Hall's pioneering novel of lesbianism, *The Well of Loneliness* (1928). Yet no censorship body in Britain had control over fiction in the same way that the BBFC had over film, and Greene was deeply unsettled by the Board's right to 'narrow so puritanically the scope of an art' (p. 16).

A few years after this attack, Greene reviewed *The Wizard of Oz* (Victor Fleming, 1939), the Technicolor adaptation of L. Frank Baum's children's book *The Wonderful Wizard of Oz* (1900). Greene suggests that to British audiences the source novel's 'morality seems a little crude and the fancy material [...] rattles like old goods' (*Spectator*, 9 February 1940, p. 371) – especially when compared to a classic British equivalent of children's literature such as Lewis Carroll's *Alice's Adventures in Wonderland* (1865). In spite of his reservations over the novel, Greene reprimands the BBFC for its decision to recommend a restrictive certificate on what is obviously a film for families with children: 'Surely it is time that this absurd committee of elderly men and spinsters who feared, too, that *Snow White* was unsuitable for those under sixteen, was laughed out of existence?' (*Spectator*, 9 February 1940, p. 371).

The Wizard of Oz was classified on 9 November 1939. It was granted a cautionary 'A' certificate, which meant that children could not be admitted unless accompanied by an adult. At the time, the decision regarding cinema admission was controlled by local councils who generally adhered to the BBFC's decisions but could exercise their own judgement: Greene's fear for *The Wizard of Oz* was that some councils would allocate the recommended 'A', so that only adults would be permitted to enter the auditorium. It was only on its re-release on 11 October 1955 that *The Wizard of Oz* was granted a 'U' certificate, permitting universal entry. Similarly, Walt Disney's *Snow White and the Seven Dwarfs* (David Hand, 1938) was initially recommended an 'A' by the BBFC, but was subsequently granted a 'U' subject to cuts being made. Indeed, the BBFC only recommended a 'U' with no cuts on its re-release in 1964.

Greene's strong views on classification and censorship, publicized in his film reviews, are echoed in his private correspondence. In a letter to V. S. Pritchett from 1948, Greene claimed that the BBFC had 'hampered the free development of films' (R. Greene, 2007, p. 158). But the BBFC was not the only authority that Greene had in his sights. In a review of August 1938, Greene discusses the re-issue of a film from earlier in the decade, *I Cover the Waterfront* (James Cruze, 1933) – an adaptation of the novel of the same name by the American author Max Miller. Greene celebrates the film because it comes 'from a period before the Hays dictatorship – when it was still just possible that the films might have become an adult art' (R. Greene, 2007, p. 260). Greene is referring here to the Motion Picture Production Code – popularly known as the Hays Code after its creator Will H. Hays – which imposed 'moral' guidelines on the US film industry (Brooke, 2010). Although the code was introduced in March 1930, it took a few years for this form of censorship to gather momentum; Greene contends that if *I Cover the Waterfront* was made now, it 'would never pass' (R. Greene, 2007, p. 158). For Greene, the powers of censorship could do nothing but slow the development of the film industry and fatally limit cinema's rich potential as a serious art form.

As we have seen with the *Frankenstein* franchise, Greene frequently condemns the popular film industry for its cynical tendency – one increasingly familiar in our own cultural moment – to adapt and remake. He dislikes *Beau Geste* (William A. Wellman, 1939), judging the film 'morbid' and appealing 'to the worst in human nature' (*Spectator*, 11 August 1939, p. 371). What distresses Greene just as much is that this is the second screen adaptation of P. C. Wren's 1924 novel, following Herbert Brenon's 1926 film, and that there are surely more to follow: 'we have not yet reached the end of *Beau Geste*; Technicolor and stereoscopy wait another decade' (p. 371). It would take longer than Greene expected: the next adaptation of the novel – written and directed by Douglas Heyes – was not released until 1966. Yet this takes nothing away from Greene's point that the technical developments in cinema were not being matched by a corresponding sophistication in its approach to its source materials.

Greene's review of *The Three Musketeers* (Allan Dwan, 1939) is suffused with a similar uneasiness. Alexandre Dumas's popular classic *Les Trois Mousquetaires* (1844) has, over time, become an 'old drab of stage and screen' (*Spectator*, 14 April 1939, p. 282), which, in its current incarnation, is unendurable for 'more than half an hour' (p. 282). Greene finds the adaptation industry producing travesties, and in his use here of the Shakespearean slang for 'prostitute' ('drab'), unambiguously underlines the purely economic motives he felt were behind it. He seems personally affronted by the adaptation of Robert Louis Stevenson's *Kidnapped* (Alfred Werker, 1938), which has excised all the adventure and nuance of character of the novel, leaving nothing but 'an odd echo – familiar names misused, lines out of the book misplaced, trivial incidents, which any competent scenarist would have cut, dragged in to take the place of – everything' (*Spectator*, 5 August 1938, p. 259). Similarly, Greene finds *Elephant Boy* (Robert J. Flaherty and Zoltan Korda, 1937), adapted from the 'Toomai of the Elephants' section of Rudyard Kipling's *The Jungle Book* (1894), to be 'faltering and repetitive' – except when actual dialogue from the original fiction is deployed with the consequence that 'the ear is caught and the attention held' (*Spectator*, 16 April 1937, pp. 192–3).

Greene also felt that adaptations could be marred when a cultural transformation is implemented on a source text, such as when a classic of Russian literature was adapted by Hollywood. The US version of Fyodor Dostoevsky's celebrated 1866 novel *Crime and Punishment* (Josef Von Sternberg, 1936) is 'vulgar as only the great New World can be vulgar, with the vulgarity of the completely unreligious, of sentimental idealism, of pitch-pine ethics, with the hollow optimism about human nature, of a salesman who has never failed to sell his canned beans' (*Spectator*, 20 March 1936, pp. 85–6). However, before we regard Greene as a conservative critic who by reflex falls prey to the cliché that the film pales in comparison with the book from which it is adapted, he is not wholly against adaptations. Although he does not enjoy *King Solomon's Mines* (Robert Stevenson, 1937), adapted from H. Rider Haggard's 1885 adventure novel of the same name, he acknowledges that this latest film version makes him 'look back with regret to the old silent picture which was faithful to Haggard's story' (*Night and Day*, 12 August 1937, p. 213). As with his politics, Greene's film reviews suggest a contrarian, shifting outlook.

Greene's reviews are distinguished not just for his frequently witty, always strong opinions, but also for his scope and frame of reference. Let us take, for instance, his appraisal of one of the most famous actresses of the era, Greta Garbo (*Night and Day*, 23 December 1937, p. 246). He begins the review by acknowledging that Garbo is 'the finest filly of them all', but complains that 'a dreadful inertia always falls on me before a new Garbo film.' There is no questioning of Garbo's acting ability: 'A great actress – oh, undoubtedly, one wearily assents, but what dull pompous films they make for her.' To develop his argument, Greene draws upon and extends a wide range of reference and allusion, but with the same economy that characterized his fiction. For example, in a single paragraph of fewer than two hundred words, Greene makes three literary references: to Thomas Carlyle's novel *Sartor Resartus* (1836), to Jonathan Swift's *Gulliver's Travels* (1726) – Greene makes Garbo an intelligent horse – a 'Houyhnhnm' among mere 'Yahoos' – and to Shakespeare's *The Winter's Tale* (1623). Using the same concision and brevity, Greene demonstrates an impressive grasp of theatre history when he refers to two *grand dames* of the melodramatic theatre, the Italian actress Eleonora Duse (1858–1924) and the French actress 'Rachel' (1821–58): Greene speculates about how Garbo will be received in the future – looking back, as it were, in order to look forward. Greene also demonstrates an impressive knowledge of film history (while playfully suggesting his lack of it), citing Garbo's various romantic encounters with John Gilbert in films such as *Flesh and the Devil* (Clarence Brown, 1926) and *Queen Christina* (Rouben Mamoulian, 1933), through to the recent offerings *Anna Karenina* (Clarence Brown, 1935) with Fredric March, *Camille* (George Cukor, 1936) with Robert Taylor and *Marie Walewska* (Clarence Brown, 1937) with Charles Boyer. In amongst this, we also find Greene's distinctive voice: Garbo was already a cult figure, a living icon of Hollywood, and yet with a typically mischievous wit and honesty, Greene suggests this mare-headed Houyhnhnm may be talented and magnificent but – to extend his terms – usually appears in films that are worthy, but not worth seeing.

Unfortunately, Greene's corpus of insightful, incisive reviews is overshadowed by the notoriety surrounding one particular episode, centring on another established star of the day: the Hollywood child superstar Shirley Temple. Reviewing the 'sentimental' yet 'a little depraved' film *Captain January* (David Butler, 1936), Greene provocatively claimed that Temple's 'popularity seems to rest on a coquetry quite as mature as Miss [Claudette] Colbert's and on an oddly precocious body as voluptuous in grey flannel trousers as Miss [Marlene] Dietrich's' (*Spectator*, 7 August 1936, p. 128). Although Greene seemed to get away with this, things came to a head the following year when he was sued by Twentieth Century Fox over his comments about Temple's appearance in *Wee Willie Winkie* (John Ford, 1937), an adaptation of another Kipling story, in the magazine *Night and Day*. Temple was still only eight years old at the time but was already Hollywood royalty, having received an Academy Award in 1935. The heart of the controversy lay in this sentence in Greene's review:

> Her admirers – middle-aged men and clergymen – respond to her dubious coquetry, to the sight of her well-shaped and desirable little body, packed with enormous vitality, only because the safety curtain of story and dialogue drops between their intelligence and their desire. (*Night and Day*, 28 October 1937, p. 234)

Greene is not just hinting that Temple appeals to paedophiles but – in that telling phrase 'dubious coquetry' – also appears to suggest that the appeal is deliberate. The resulting court case went against Greene and saw a crippling fine extracted from *Night and Day*, of which Greene was co-founder and editor, as well as a contributor. It led to the magazine's collapse soon after, and left Greene financially bruised and embittered by the affair.

Greene's film reviews were characterized by a profound insight into form, genre and performance, married with a distinctive voice that was as typically incisive as it was acerbic (and in the case of the Shirley Temple furore, destructive). Eventually Greene's interests would lead him away from reviewing but, as we have seen, these few years immersed in the auditorium gave him a considerable education, as Greene himself acknowledged, and his reviews would in turn provide an education for subsequent generations of film critics. Indeed, his reviews remain as rewarding now, as then: he offers detailed points of aesthetic focus and analysis but is also able extend this to the appraisal of wider social, cultural or historical issues. He attempts to make the reader look more widely – and critically – at the mechanisms of adaptation and at the film industry and its regulation, most significantly on the point of censorship, as we have seen. As Norman Sherry explains: 'Greene's long fascination with the cinema aroused in him extremes of emotional response and a deeply critical attitude towards films, their makers and those who appeared in them' (Sherry,

1989, p. 587). Sherry hereby captures another of the essential ambiguities of Greene: he is, at one and the same time, fascinated by cinema and yet scornful of what it produces.

Exercises

- Look at contemporary film reviews in newspapers, magazines or other forums. What can they tell us about the place of film in wider culture and society? What can they tell us about the place of adaptation in film? What attitudes towards adaptation are apparent in these reviews?
- Look at Greene's reviews and those of his contemporaries and consider how they engage with the cinema of their time.
- Philip French, the long-serving critic for the *Observer*, has underlined the influence of Greene's film criticism on his own. Can you find any traces of Greene's film criticism in the film reviews of today?

Chapter Two

The Carol Reed Films

In the history of cinema, legends and cults can develop around certain creative partnerships. This is most apparent in the relationship between directors and actors: in the context of US cinema we might think of the association of the directors Tim Burton, Quentin Tarantino and Woody Allen with the actors Johnny Depp, Samuel L. Jackson and Diane Keaton, respectively, in a range of films spanning the late 1960s through to the present day. In the context of European cinema, we might consider the fiery yet fertile relationship between the director Werner Herzog and the actor Klaus Kinski in the New German Cinema, or the French New Wave director François Truffaut's use of the actor Jean-Pierre Léaud in a number of semi-autobiographical films spanning some twenty years. Aside from these high-profile actor–director partnerships, we could consider the successful creative partnerships between the director Alfred Hitchcock and the composer Bernard Herrmann or between the director Martin Scorsese and the editor Thelma Schoonmaker.

When it comes to a creative partnership between a writer and a director, one that has acquired a particular reputation is that which exists between Graham Greene and Carol Reed. Surprisingly, this partnership is based on just three films: *The Fallen Idol* (1948), *Our Man in Havana* (1959) and, most famously, *The Third Man* (1949). Even more surprisingly, perhaps, the reputation of this partnership arguably rests on just one film. Their final collaboration, *Our Man in Havana*, is at best a rather disappointing, uneven comedy. And although their first collaboration *The Fallen Idol* was the only time Greene was Oscar-nominated for a screenplay and remains a highly impressive example of British cinema and adaptation (and Greene's favourite among all his film scripts [Sherry, 1994, p. 241]), it is also a somewhat neglected film. Both of these films are eclipsed by their second collaboration, *The Third Man*. *The Third Man* has acquired a truly monolithic status. It was a box-office hit and winner of the Grand Prix at Cannes on its release in 1949, and to the present day continues to be regarded as the 'greatest' British film in definitive surveys for the British Film Institute and in other widely respected forums. Given that *The Third Man* is a lead contender as the 'quintessential' British film as well as a milestone in the history of cinema more broadly, it is perhaps inevitable that the stories and rumours that surrounded its creation have become legendary: images and characters have become iconic, while lines of dialogue, the soundtrack and the title itself have acquired mythic status. In addition, the film continues to be a case study that affords multiple readings and a diverse range of analytical approaches. While this chapter will devote significant attention to *The Third Man*, the film that anyone interested in Greene and cinema is obliged to view, it will also give some attention to the other Reed-Greene films, so marginalized by the story of Harry Lime and post-War Vienna – from *The Fallen Idol* and *Our Man in Havana*, to a Reed-Greene collaboration that never was, *No Man's Land* (1950).

The Fallen Idol

Greene's screenplay for *The Fallen Idol* was based on his 1935 short story 'The Basement Room', which first appeared in the *News Chronicle* and was later collected in *Twenty-One Stories* (1954). The story centres on a small boy called Philip Lane, who has been left alone in the family home for a few days while his parents are away, in the care of the family butler Baines and his housekeeper wife Mrs Baines. The story is told through the eyes of the young Philip, and this point-of-view is implicit in the naming of the butler and his wife – 'Baines' and 'Mrs Baines' being the only names by which the seven-year-old son of their employer knows (or would dare to address) them. Philip idolizes Baines, and Baines is clearly fond of him in turn, lavishing the lonely child (whom in a sign of their closeness he affectionately calls 'Phil') with treats and tales of his days in Africa. By contrast, Mrs Baines is a spiteful and harrying presence, and attempts to befriend the boy not from affection, but as an unwitting informant on her husband's suspected infidelity. One day, Philip surprises Baines and his much younger lover Emmy at a seedy Pimlico teashop.

Philip has the misapprehension – encouraged by Baines – that Emmy is his niece, and discovery and, with it, domestic upheaval appear to have been averted. Baines asks Philip to keep the rendezvous secret, but the bullying Mrs Baines manages to extract the information from the child, and swears him to secrecy in turn. She pretends to go away, luring Baines into inviting Emmy to stay the night, and during the night appears frighteningly at Philip's bedside, demanding to know where the lovers are. Philip screams out a warning, and during the ensuing confrontation and struggle with her husband, she topples – or is toppled (it remains unclear) – over the banisters 'in a flurry of black clothes' (*Fallen Idol*, p. 122), falling to her death. Panicked, Philip rushes out into the garden and then into street, and, having become lost, is brought home by a policeman. Philip inadvertently betrays the fact that the body of Mrs Baines has been moved, alerting the policeman to the possibility of foul play. As the policeman begins his interrogation, the narrative flashes forward several decades, as Philip, now an old man on his deathbed, and clearly still traumatized by these events from his childhood, finds himself reliving them as he slips slowly into unconsciousness.

When the story was published Greene was arguably as much a travel-writer as a novelist, and would go on to produce two classics of the genre, *Journey Without Maps* (1936) and *The Lawless Roads* (1939). In fact, both of these works of non-fiction are intrinsic to his career as a writer of literary fiction, and suggestively underscore Greene's capacity for self-adaptation. *The Lawless Roads*, about religious purges in the Tobasco region of Mexico during the 1930s, would go on to inform his 1940 novel come parable, *The Power and the Glory*. Meanwhile *Journey Without Maps*, about his trek through the hinterland of the then-comparatively unknown West African country Liberia, was the first substantial commitment to paper of Greene's love affair with Africa, which also informs well-known longer works such as *The Heart of the Matter* (1948) and *A Burnt-Out Case* (1961), less well-known shorter ones such as 'A Chance for Mr Lever' (1936), and unfinished ones such as the story fragment 'The Other Side of the Border' (c. 1936). This recurrent fascination with Africa can also be felt in the figure of Baines, who appears to have had a previous life as a colonialist in Sierra Leone, the scene of both *Journey Without Maps* and *The Heart of the Matter*. Indeed, though set in London rather than Africa, 'The Basement Room' springs from the same imaginative vein as these works, being 'conceived on the cargo steamer on the way home' after his African trek, as Greene later commented, in order 'to relieve the tedium of the voyage' (Preface, *FI*, p. 101). In this particular story, however, Greene is thinking less of colonialism than class relations. Baines was a man of some power abroad (at least according to his self-mythologizing reminiscences) but a subordinate at home, and the original title of the story, 'The Basement Room', captures something of the 'upstairs-downstairs' architecture of class relations in pre-war Britain.

Beyond this, the story's key themes of betrayal and infidelity, with lethal consequences, are ones which reverberate throughout Greene's literary corpus, from his debut novel *The Man Within* (1929) to *The Heart of the Matter* (1948), *The Third Man* (1950), *The End of the Affair* (1951), *The Quiet American* (1955), *The Comedians* (1966) and *The Honorary Consul* (1973), to name only several examples. Mrs Baines's stairwell death anticipates that of one of the main characters in Greene's next major novel, *Brighton Rock* (1938), another story which centres on a damaged youth. In fact, childhood trauma is another familiar trope, and when Greene was not exploring this in his fiction – from early works such as his 1929 short tale 'The End of the Party' (also collected in *Twenty-One Stories*) through to middle and late works such as 'Under the Garden' (from 1961's *A Sense of Reality*) and *The Captain and the Enemy* (1988) – he was exploring it in autobiography, *A Sort of Life* (1971) being written on doctor's orders, 'as a form of therapy' (Allain, 1983, p. 15). Similarly, the green baize door which separates the basement kitchen from the main house, and through which the young Philip ventures after his parents have left, is a recurrent motif in Greene's work – a border that is both psychological and physical – and can be traced back to his schooldays at Berkhamsted school, where his father was headmaster: 'a green baize door separated the safe familial home from the threatening corridors and dormitories of the school where the young Greene, as the head's son, was subject to bullying and exclusion' (Lodge, 2006). In this way, it marks the original 'dangerous edge' which Greene, borrowing from Robert Browning, volunteered as an epigraph for his works as a whole. In this story in particular, it marks the threshold from innocence into experience and disillusionment, bringing the young boy who crosses it into irrevocable contact with the adult world, and with it, illicit passion and possible murder.

Beyond these consonances with his own literary corpus, 'The Basement Room' has much in common with the works of other authors. The narrative is focalized through the eyes of a small and naïvely uncomprehending child, and in this regard it follows in the tradition of *What Maisie Knew* (1897) by Henry James, another of Greene's literary mentors, and can be seen as a forerunner to L. P. Hartley's *The Go-Between* (1953) and even Jonathan Safran Foer's *Everything is Illuminated* (2002) and Mark Haddon's *The Curious Incident of the Dog in the Night-time* (2003), themselves the subjects of classic and recent well-regarded screen and stage adaptations. These are stories in which a single, lonely and neglected child is focal to the narrative and whose world of innocence is brought into contact with and shattered by the unforgiving realities of the adult world. They are, then, stories of the hurtful inauguration into the world of 'experience', and like 'The Basement Room' are structurally interesting insofar as the central child character frequently does not share the comprehension of the reader. There is also a thematic link between 'The Basement Room' and James's Gothic masterpiece *The Turn of the Screw* (1898), inasmuch as both works concern the oppressive domestic environment of privileged children and their complex (and perhaps Oedipal) relationships with servants. (James's ghostly novella also figures in Greene's 'The End of the Party', in which a boy is literally frightened to death.)

Just as there are overlaps and appropriations between the original story and other literary works, so, too, are there obvious echoes between *The Fallen Idol* and contemporary cinema, from comic or musical films featuring children in central roles, such as those of Greene's *bête noir* Shirley Temple, to dramatic works such as *These Three* (William Wyler, 1936), a film much admired by Greene (Sinyard, 2003, p. 55), or *Angels with Dirty Faces* (Michael Curtiz, 1938). *The Fallen Idol* also bears comparison to two contemporary European neorealist films, *Bicycle Thieves* (Vittorio de Sica, 1948) and *Germany Year Zero* (Roberto Rossellini, 1948). *Bicycle Thieves* is set and filmed in post-war Rome and presents the desperate search of a man (played by Lamberto Maggiorani) and his son (Enzo Staiola) for the stolen bicycle upon which the family's already precarious livelihood depends. The film features an exquisitely realized and convincingly portrayed relationship between the two central actors. *Germany Year Zero* was likewise made on location, this time in the ruins of post-war Berlin, and is likewise focalized through the eyes of a young boy (Edmund Moeschke) as he attempts to eke out an existence through petty crime, but falls victim to black marketeers and sexual exploitation. Like *The Fallen Idol* and *Bicycle Thieves*, *Germany Year Zero* is distinguished by an extraordinary central performance from a child actor.

When 'The Basement Room' appeared in 1935, Greene was the newly appointed film critic for the *Spectator*, and in one of his early reviews had praised Reed's *Midshipman Easy* (1935), an adaptation of Frederick Marryat's 1836 Napoleonic adventure novel. Greene had provocatively suggested that Reed – who like himself was still a relative fledgling in his chosen craft – 'had more sense of the cinema than most veteran British directors' (*Spectator*, 3 January 1936, p. 18). Since then, Reed had gone on to make his name in the British studio system with films such as *The Stars Look Down* (1940), an adaptation of A. J. Cronin's novel, several propaganda works made during the Second World War, including *The Way Ahead* (1944), and, just after it, the acclaimed thriller *Odd Man Out* (1947). Similarly, Greene had found some measure of financial success after selling the film rights to the thriller *Stamboul Train* (1932), and had cemented his reputation as an author of popular and yet highly accomplished literary works such as *Brighton Rock* (1938), adapted for the screen by John and Roy Boulting in 1947. For his part, Reed also wanted to adapt Greene – but 'The Basement Room' was not his initial choice: he had been considering the Sweden-set novel *England Made Me* (1935), when the producer Alexander Korda had instead suggested 'The Basement Room' as a source. Reed read the story, and immediately fell for it. A meeting with Greene was swiftly arranged, and the project – and the beginnings of a fruitful and highly regarded working partnership – was born. As David Lodge notes, '*The Fallen Idol* was a model of what the development of a movie should be, but very seldom is: a close collaboration between a writer and a director who enjoyed complete rapport, supported by a producer', in Korda, 'who did not interfere with the creative process' (Lodge, 2006).

It was here that the pattern of their future collaborations took shape. As Greene later recalled, he and Reed took three interconnecting rooms at the Metropole Hotel in Brighton, one for each of them, with a secretary taking the middle room. Greene worked during the mornings while Reed slept late, and they discussed the progress of the script over lunch (Falk, 2000, p. 104). The screenplay was completed in four months, between June and September 1947, with Greene using as much of his original dialogue as he could for the film version before this was 'slowly whittled down to reduce the dialogue as much as possible' (Sherry, 1994, p. 241). Working closely with Reed, Greene took the powerful dramatic essence of 'The Basement Room' and made several decisions – some small, some radical – which would serve to enhance the cinematic version. These are chiefly to do with plot and narrative – the complexity of the latter being one of the reasons why Greene had initially felt that the work was 'unfilmable' (Preface, *FI*, p. 101).

In the original story – and in keeping with the dubious moral terrain of Greene's fiction from the period, where cold-blooded killers such as Raven in *A Gun For Sale* (1936) and Pinkie in *Brighton Rock* are also objects of the reader's sympathy, if not empathy – it is left tantalisingly unclear whether Mrs Baines's death is an accident. For the screenplay, however, Greene and Reed considered the culpability of the likable Baines difficult to pull off on film, and 'would certainly have imperilled the £250,000 that films nowadays cost' (Preface, *FI*, p. 101). Instead, they made Baines (played by Ralph Richardson) innocent of murdering his wife: as in his story to the police, she has indeed slipped to her death accidentally (here, from an outdoor ledge from which she was trying to spy on Baines and his lover, who is now named Julie, and who is now one of the typists whose legs Philip glimpses through the basement window in the original story). This produces a significant shift of dramatic emphasis in the denouement: in the original story, Philip's unwary remarks put Baines in the dock accidentally, but for a crime he may have committed; in the film, he wrongly believes his friend Baines to be a murderer and, telling lies in his defence, almost incriminates an innocent man. Crucially, however – and in stark contrast to the original ending – none of the grown-ups believes the boy, and Baines is vindicated and happily reunited with his beloved, as is the boy with his returning parents. Baines is, however, still not quite all that he seems to be. In the original story, Baines's anecdotes about his time in Africa, though self-aggrandizing, ring true, but in the film they are clearly fictitious, and at the end he is forced to admit that he has never even been there. A pet snake was also introduced, of which Mrs Baines (played by Sonia Dresdel) nurses a particular hatred, and which, in an act freighted with symbolism, she eventually kills. Thus the main crime of the story, the possible murder of Mrs Baines, is replaced by a series of smaller 'crimes' – the secrets, lies and suspicions which, taken together, chip away at the young protagonist's necessary trust in the adults around him, and allow him to believe that a murder may have been committed. Equally, the boy remains the person through whom the narrative is focalized but does not, as in the original story, have any corresponding authorial power to shape events, wittingly or not: he is just a child, whose 'story' none of the adults believe.

In the original story there are several authorial interpolations. On one level, these give the reader a greater understanding of a particular episode or exchange, the significance of which is lost on Philip, through whose eyes it is apprehended; for instance, when Baines asks the boy not to mention the girl, Emmy, to Mrs Baines: "'Of course not", Philip said [...] "I understand, Baines." But he didn't understand a thing; he was caught up in other people's darkness' (*FI*, p. 111). On another level, there are two narrative 'flash-forwards', where the same authorial voice interrupts to comment on the action sixty years hence: the deathbed scene upon which the story ends and another where it is revealed that Philip, given a Meccano set by Mrs Baines as a bribe, 'never opened his Meccano set again, never built anything, never created anything, died, the old dilettante, sixty years later with nothing to show rather than preserve the memory of Mrs Baines's malicious voice saying good night, her soft determined footfalls on the stairs to the basement, going down, going down' (*FI*, p. 114).

Although these authorial intrusions might easily have been accommodated, they are done away with in the film. The original story was a dark psychological study of childhood trauma, the impact of which is revealed in the final sentences, but with the removal of these analepses where this trauma is excavated and revealed, this Freudian element – the emblematic snake aside – is diminished (though the Oedipal nature of the relationship between the boy and those in whose care he has been entrusted is played up, with his parents removed for longer than the two weeks specified in the original, and the boy unable to remember his mother as a result – a role which Mrs Baines ominously now fills). Instead, the film eschews the effects of childhood trauma to emphasize the sense of loss that comes from leaving childish things behind: this is just a rite of passage, rather than something formative and damaging. In its place is a Hitchcockian tale of drama and suspense, with a 'happy' ending of romantic reunion and domestic harmony (of a sort) restored, replacing the doubly bleak and narratologically complex ending of the original: Baines confessing to the crime, overlaid with Philip's deathbed struggle to come to terms with its impact sixty years on. The point-of-view aspect of the original, however, is retained, and this gives the film its particular edge. As David Lodge notes, Reed utilizes the interior of the house to emphasize 'the isolation and vulnerability of the little boy [...] who so often observes the adult world from a distance: from high landings and balconies, between banisters, and through windows' (Lodge, 2006).

Similarly, the boy is shown to glimpse the action surrounding the death of Mrs Baines in stages, through windows on different levels as he flees the house down the fire escape, and it is this series of partial perspectives that leads him to believe that Baines *has* murdered his wife.

More obviously, the setting was changed from a palatial house in Belgravia to the Embassy of an unspecified francophone country (with 'Philip', played by Bobby Henrey, becoming 'Philippe') and the title from 'The Basement Room' to 'The Fallen Idol'. Greene felt the shift in setting made the story more plausibly contemporary (few households would have had butlers in the austerity of post-war England), but disliked the new title, which was chosen by the distributors. As is common among writers who adapt their own work, and who are as a result more protective of the integrity of their 'original' text, Greene felt that the change was unnecessary, and that the new title was 'meaningless' (Preface, *FI*, p. 101) in the context of the story. That said, it does gesture to the high esteem in which Philippe has held Baines, and to which Baines has failed to live up (an alternative title was 'The Lost Illusion'). Equally, Greene claimed that the new title 'always reminded me of the problem paintings of John Collier' (Preface, *FI*, p. 101). This was a genre of art popular during the late-Victorian era, the most celebrated example of which was William Frederick Yeames's *'And When Did You Last See Your Father?'* (1878), which, like Greene's story, centres on a young child being quizzed by the authorities, who, like Greene's protagonist, is on the cusp of betraying someone to whom he is close. More broadly, the genre featured a similar narrative ambiguity as that which characterizes Greene's story, especially in the uncertainty over what has happened to Mrs Baines. As all of this suggests, the new title is if anything *more* germane than the original – because of, rather than despite, Greene's objections. This cavil aside, he retained a high regard for the film itself – and even preferred it to its more illustrious successor, *The Third Man* – his next collaboration with Reed.

On its release in 1948, *The Fallen Idol* was popular both at the box office and with the critics. One of the highest grossing British pictures of that year, it was nominated for two Academy Awards (Best Director for Reed; Best Adapted Screenplay for Greene) and won a BAFTA for Best British Film, along with numerous garlands in Europe and elsewhere (including awards for Best Screenplay at the prestigious Venice Film Festival and for Best Director by the equally prestigious New York Film Critics Circle). Richardson delivers a performance of delicately realized warmth and empathy as Baines, supported by the deliciously wicked Dresdel as Mrs Baines. Even more crucial to the film's success was the casting and direction of Bobby Henrey as Philippe, through whom most of the story is focalized, and upon whom its dramatic effectiveness greatly depends, and it is here that Reed's direction, fêted by the critics, comes to the fore. As Quentin Falk glosses:

> In the finished film of 94 minutes' duration, smooth as it seems to the uninitiated, there is a total of 1,040 separate splices. Although the audience thinks of [Henrey] as an integral part of the entire drama, actually he plays most of his scenes alone. Sometimes he is seen walking beside Baines. The coats and the trousers of Baines, however, are Carol Reed's. (Falk, 2000, p. 56)

As Falk underlines, Reed worked extensively and closely with the eight-year-old Henrey, away from the rest of the cast and crew, explaining and demonstrating every move and emotion, thus enabling, through a meticulous and technical process, the authentic performance we see on the screen – a process which can also be seen to anticipate the 'blue screen' methods prevalent in modern-day, CGI-heavy productions, whereby actors work ostensibly alone with the director. The skewed point-of-view shots and Philippe's dash through haunting night-time streets (which again are shot through with his perspective) also anticipate the landmark expressionist cinematography of Reed and Greene's next film, *The Third Man*. In this way, although *The Third Man* remains their most celebrated collaboration, not to mention one of the defining landmarks of twentieth-century British cinema, *The Fallen Idol* remains a hugely significant work.

Exercises

- The title of 'The Basement Room' was changed in the adaptation to *The Fallen Idol*. Identify some other examples of adaptation where the title has been changed. What (if anything) is lost in this alteration? And what is gained?
- How might the 'flash forward' episodes in the original story have been accommodated in film? How might this affect the timeline of the main story? Can you identify examples of how this might be done from elsewhere in cinema?

- Consider how the events of the story could be mediated from the perspective of Baines, Mrs Baines or Emmy.
- Compare *The Fallen Idol* with other films which centre on children and feature journeys from innocence to experience, such as *The Go-Between* (Joseph Losey, 1970), *Germany Year Zero* (Roberto Rossellini, 1948) and *What Maisie Knew* (Scott McGehee, 2012).

The Third Man

The Third Man (1950) is set in occupied Vienna shortly after the end of the Second World War. It focuses upon Rollo Martins, a writer of pulp Westerns, who has travelled to Vienna at the invitation of an old school-friend Harry Lime, an employee of the International Refugee Office, to write about refugees. On his arrival Martins discovers that Lime has been killed in a car accident, and, after his suspicions are aroused by the mysterious presence of a 'third man' at the scene of his friend's death, he decides to investigate. Although penniless, he is mistaken for another visiting author by the British Council, who invite him to stay on in Vienna at their expense, enabling him to carry out his detective work. He gradually learns that Lime faked his own death to elude capture by the British authorities, and that Lime is a black market racketeer who has been selling adulterated penicillin, which has killed or driven insane many of the city's hospital patients (many of them children). Martins reluctantly agrees to help the British forces capture Lime, and during a pursuit through the city's underground sewers, shoots and kills Lime. During all of this, Martins falls in love with Lime's mistress, Anna Schmidt. She has fewer illusions about Lime than Martins, but remains loyal to him until the end. At Lime's second (and real) funeral, she is seen departing arm-in-arm with Martins. The story is related by Major Calloway of the British Army police, and is 'reconstructed [...] from my own files and from what Martins told me' (*Third Man*, p. 7). The novella ends as it begins, with the funeral of Lime.

Though set in contemporary Vienna, the story's personal and political terrains are recognizably those of 'Greeneland'. There is the familiar quest of one male character for another to whom he is emotionally attached, in often dangerous circumstances, which culminates in betrayal and death, as in Greene's first novel *The Man Within* (1929). There is also the added complication of a female love interest and a moral justification of the betrayal of a friend that is qualified by the desire for his mistress, as in his later novel *The Quiet*

American (1955). (The recurrence of such love triangles in Greene's work during the period is also in some ways a reflection of Greene's troubled personal life, in particular his jealous and obsessive passion for Catherine Walston – the model for Sarah Miles in his next major work *The End of the Affair* [1951] – with whom he had begun an affair shortly before coming to write *The Third Man*.) There is even a characteristic nod to Greene's mentor Joseph Conrad. Reed had approached Greene to write the screenplay of an adaptation of Conrad's second novel *An Outcast of the Islands* (1896), but Greene – feeling too much in thrall to Conrad – declined, and Reed later made the film without his help. Nevertheless, Conrad's presence can be felt in *The Third Man*, most obviously in the shape of a character called Kurtz, the anti-hero of Conrad's most celebrated and controversial work, *Heart of Darkness* (1899).

There are also structural similarities between *The Third Man* and *Heart of Darkness*. Both follow the path of a naïve outsider as he ventures into a dangerous realm in search of a man who has been held in high esteem but who has suffered a fall from grace. Anna, who has no illusions about her lover Lime, appears far removed from the naïve and doting figure of Kurtz's Intended in *Heart of Darkness*, but like the Intended she has an essential function in defining – even sealing – the fateful journey of the story's main male protagonist. The memorable and disturbing final solution put forward by Kurtz in *Heart of Darkness*, 'Exterminate all the brutes!', meanwhile, is echoed in a similar expression of inhumanity put forward by Lime to a shocked Martins as they survey the crowds of people below Vienna's Great Wheel: "'Would you really feel any pity if one of those dots stopped moving – for ever?'" (*TM*, p. 86). Greene also uses snow like Conrad uses the jungle in *Heart of Darkness*, to suggest an impenetrable carapace (literally so in a Vienna where 'the gravediggers had [...] to use electric drills to open the frozen ground' [*TM*, p. 6]) that reflects the 'impenetrable mystery' surrounding the main protagonist's attempt to locate the truth. Equally, the 'river of darkness', where the main protagonist in Conrad's tale finally encounters Kurtz, corresponds to *The Third Man*'s underground sewers where Martins has his final encounter with Lime (Watts, 1997, p. 194). These overlaps between *The Third Man* and *Heart of Darkness* can also be felt in the subsequent film of Greene's novella. Its co-star Orson Welles had passionately desired to adapt Conrad's work for the screen, and had written a screenplay in the late 1930s; when this was rejected by the producers RKO, Welles instead made his masterpiece, *Citizen Kane* (1941).

The specific choice of Vienna as a setting is crucial to the story, with the divided loyalties of its main characters reflected in the new political geography of a city which (like post-war Berlin) has been 'divided up in zones among the Four Powers' of Britain, France, America and the Soviet Union (*TM*, p. 6), and is now torn, as a result, between East and West. This is no longer the legendary, baroque capital of fame and song – 'the Old Vienna' of Strauss, the Danube, Sacher's Hotel, the Kärntnerstrasse and the Prater, as the narrator underlines (*TM*, p. 7); instead, it is a city devastated by war and its aftermath, scarred not only by ruins but also by racketeering and kidnappings – a kind of modern 'frontier' equivalent to the one featured in the Wild West tales from which Martins makes a living, as well as a frontline of the early Cold War. The story hereby displays Greene's characteristic fascination with borders and border crossings, both real and imagined. Lime's criminal underworld is a literal one, comprising the sewers underneath the city, which are not – unlike the world above ground – divided among or policed by the occupying powers, and which complement Lime's moral descent and disregard of boundaries of a legal or ethical sort. The narrator even goes as far as linking Lime's criminality to that of the city's now deposed or dead fascist leaders, when he asserts that a 'racket works very like a totalitarian party' (*TM*, p. 63). As well as sharing some of the common topography of 'Greeneland', Greene's Vienna is also a place in and of itself. The story not only gives the 'impression [...] of the background' (*TM*, p. 6) promised by the narrator, but also a fully realized portrait of post-war Vienna. Indeed, from its opening description of the city's famous landmark the Prater, now strewn with weeds and rusted tanks, *The Third Man* depends to a great extent on Greene's 'incomparable ability to evoke the sense of place' (Lodge, 2005, p. x).

Such an ability to evoke place derived, in no small part, from Greene's long and close relationship with cinema. As David Lodge underlines:

> Greene belonged to the first generation of British writers who grew up with the movies, and his work, like that of his contemporaries Evelyn Waugh, Henry Green and Christopher Isherwood, was deeply influenced by the new medium. What Greene learnt from cinema was how to hold his readers in the coils of a suspenseful plot while exploring unsettling moral and metaphysical themes, and how to evoke character and milieu with the verbal equivalent of cinematic close-ups and [camera] pans. (Lodge, 2005, p. vii)

As Greene himself would later claim (Allain, 1983, pp. 132–3), whereas previous writers such as Conrad and Ford Madox Ford (another great influence on him) had also drawn on the visual arts – in particular the paintings of the Impressionists – his own work gained from cinema a sense of motion and movement that was lacking in the works of his forerunners, many of whom were suspicious of the then-new medium (Seed, 2005). Yet whereas Greene successfully borrowed from cinema, films of his fiction were rarely wholly successful. Given the sheer number of adaptations of Greene's work, this is a particularly crowded field: of the twenty-six novels and numerous short stories Greene wrote (and excluding unpublished works and television adaptations of his work), there have been almost forty films made (Barrett, 2009, p. 423).

The Third Man, however, directed by Carol Reed, and scripted by Greene himself, quickly became and has remained one of the classics of post-war British cinema, popular not only with the critics but also with the general public – its success even extending to 'The Third Man Theme' by Anton Karas, which topped the international music charts in 1950 (Watts, 1997, p. 188). The film was acclaimed on both sides of the Atlantic on its release in Britain in late 1949 and in America in early 1950, and in all parts of the press, 'from popular daily newspapers to specialist film magazines, from niche consumer publications to the broadsheet establishment papers' (White, 2012a). It won the Grand Prix at the Cannes International Film Festival and an Academy Award for cinematography, and has regularly placed highly in surveys of the best of British cinema ever since. *Stamboul Train* (1932) is notable for being the first novel of Greene's to be adapted for the screen and for providing a small but serendipitous windfall at a time when, doubting whether he could make a living from being a novelist, he had considered returning to his old job at the *Times*. The financial success of *The Third Man*, and the impact of this success on Greene's career as a writer, can be measured in similar terms: he bought a small house on the Italian island of Anacapri with the proceeds, and it was here that he wrote much of his later fiction (*WE*, p. 134).

In fact, *The Third Man* was so successful that Greene and Reed immediately embarked on another, similar film project in early 1950. It was provisionally referred to as 'The Harz Mountains Story', before being given the more Greeneian (and genre-friendly) title *No Man's Land*. The plot centres on an English spy called Brown, who, posing as a writer, has ventured into German border territories controlled by the Soviets (the 'No Man's Land' of the title) to retrieve an important microfilm. He is arrested and tortured by the Soviet secret police, and put into the hands of the Turgenev-quoting Captain Starhov, with whom he forms an unlikely bond. He also forms a romantic bond with his captor's mistress, Clara, who helps him escape to safety. It was inspired by a news story Greene had read concerning the discovery of rich deposits of uranium at Eisleben and the disturbing implications of this given the Russians' burgeoning atomic programme (Sexton, 2005, p. xviii). In this way, *No Man's Land* can be seen as a forerunner of Greene's 1958 Cold War satire *Our Man in Havana*, which he and Reed adapted for the screen in 1960 – the third and final of their collaborations.

No Man's Land was the only finished piece of extended fiction which Greene wrote between *The Third Man* and *The End of the Affair*, and in its exploration of themes of romance and betrayal acts as 'something of a sequel to the former and a "prequel" to the latter', as James Sexton has pointed out (2005, p. xiii). Yet in many ways *No Man's Land* is less a sequel to *The Third Man*, to extend Sexton's metaphor, than a remake. Like *The Third Man*, it is a mystery thriller set in occupied Europe (here Germany rather than Austria) after the end of the Second World War and at the start of the Cold War. Like *The Third Man*, it features a main character ('Brown') whose name (like 'Lime') is a punning reference to Greene himself. Like *The Third Man*, it involves the betrayal by one male character of another which results in death, and is complicated by their shared love of a woman. Like *The Third Man*, the story of the main protagonists is related by a seemingly disinterested third party, who has reconstructed the story from the accounts of its chief actors. Like *The Third Man*, it even features as a comic interlude an incongruous cultural event (with an amateur drama festival standing in for *The Third Man*'s literary symposium). In fact, *No Man's Land* resembled *The Third Man* a little too closely, and the project to film it was abandoned.

Whereas *No Man's Land* too closely resembled its predecessor, *The Third Man* itself bore several close resemblances to the real-world of espionage. Con Coroneos describes a case of what seemed to be life imitating art:

> In May 1951, the Englishmen Guy Burgess and Donald Maclean defected to the Soviet Union. The *Daily Express* [...] broke the story that the escape had been made with the help of a government insider, a shadowy "third man." The term gradually gained currency both in Britain and overseas, and when Kim Philby [Greene's former colleague in British Secret

Intelligence] was eventually named in the British Parliament in September 1955, the *Washington News* [...] led with an article entitled: "All that is needed is the Harry Lime theme music. Who was the Third Man?" (Coroneos, 2002, p. 157)

Greene later fictionalized the Philby defection to Soviet Russia in his 1978 spy novel *The Human Factor*. Coroneos suggests that Philby features much earlier in Greene's work, however, speculating that Greene suspected his colleague of being a double agent, and that his portrait of Harry Lime in *The Third Man* is a coded account of Philby himself (Coroneos, 2002, p. 158). The story's use of Vienna is interesting in this regard: Greene knew that Philby was a British Intelligence operative in Vienna during the mid-1930s, and had used the same sewers in which Lime evades detection (Coroneos, 2002, p. 158). In another case of art imitating life, Greene's location-finding trips to Prague and Vienna in 1948 were conducted under the auspices of Alexander Korda's production company London Films, 'which had been an occasional front for the SIS [Secret Intelligence Service] since the 1930s' (Coroneos, 2002, p. 158) – the same service, in other words, for which Philby and Greene had worked during the war. Moreover, as Greene would discover, *The Third Man* appeared to provoke some of the international tensions represented in it; Korda's partner David O. Selznick, for one, saw it as a piece of British propaganda (Coroneos, 2002, p. 158). This is nothing if not apt: Martins's original purpose in going to Vienna, after all, is to write propaganda on Lime's behalf. There is also another, concealed reference to propaganda in the film. The film that Martins and Anna go to see is an old 'Tom Mix' cowboy picture; Viennese cinemas were forced to screen such works because the Allied forces now occupying the city had destroyed much of the 'native' film stock, seeing it as propagandist and fearing it would have a detrimental impact on the city's post-war recovery – not to mention on how the Allied presence there was perceived. The world of espionage and the world of the writer were in a significant sense naturally complementary for Greene. As Mr Savory, the fictional author in *Stamboul Train*, acknowledges, the writer of fiction is '"a spy"', of sorts – someone who has '"to see everything and pass unnoticed"' in order to gather the raw matter for his stories (*Stamboul Train*, p. 51).

Greene's novella *The Third Man* (1950) is a compelling and exceptionally well-crafted work of fiction, and its cinematic impetus partly explains its impressive concision. Greene frequently set out to make his fiction 'cinematic' in order to attract the attention of filmmakers, most notably the early thriller *Stamboul Train*, which was bought by Twentieth Century Fox and filmed as *Orient Express* in 1934. Yet although *The Third Man* preceded and formed the basis of the ensuing film adaptation, the novella itself was never intended for publication: 'My film story [...] was never written to be read but only to be seen', as Greene put it (Preface, *TM*, p. 122). Like the unfilmed stories *The Tenth Man* (1944) and *No Man's Land*, or the unfinished fragment *The Stranger's Hand* (the basis of a 1954 film directed by Mario Soldati starring *The Third Man*'s Trevor Howard and Alida Valli), *The Third Man* instead began life as a film 'treatment'. As David Lodge explains, a 'film treatment is usually a detailed summary of what the proposed film would actually show.' Yet 'Greene's treatments are formally indistinguishable from his short stories' because they 'include many touches' – most notably the use of abstract metaphor and simile characteristic of all of Greene's fiction – 'that would be impossible to replicate in the film medium' (Lodge, 2005, p. viii). Nevertheless, such treatments had a particular usefulness for Greene. As he puts it in the Preface to *The Third Man*, published following the enormous success of the film: 'To me it is almost impossible to write a film play without first writing a story. Even a film depends on more than plot, on a certain measure of characterization, on mood and atmosphere', 'and these seem to me almost impossible to capture for the first time in the dull shorthand of a script' (Preface, *TM*, p. 3). Moreover, though formally indistinguishable from his short stories, a film treatment such as *The Third Man* differs from these stories because it does not represent the final state of the text to be adapted; rather, it is merely 'the raw material' for the film itself, which, as Greene underlines, 'is in this case the finished state of the story' (Preface, *TM*, p. 4).

The origins of the story were likewise a collaborative affair. Having enjoyed producing Reed and Greene's *The Fallen Idol*, Korda pressed Greene for an outline for a further film. As he recounts in *Ways of Escape* (1980), Greene in return came up with a single sentence about the apparent resurrection of a man thought dead and buried, scrawled 'on the flap of an envelope': '"I had paid my last farewell to Harry a week ago, when his coffin was lowered into the frozen February ground, so that it was with incredulity I saw him pass by, without a sign of recognition, among the host of strangers in the Strand"' (*WE*, p. 122). The idea for the story's setting, postwar occupied Vienna, meanwhile, was also Korda's (Watts, 1997, p. 189). Korda's reasons for choosing Vienna were largely pragmatic.

Echoing the currency problems faced by Martins on his arrival in Vienna, London Films had certain reserves of currency in Austria, and this was a time when currency exchange was difficult, requiring permission from the government and central banks (White, 2012b). It made financial sense, therefore, to film on location in Vienna. Korda's partner in the production, David O. Selznick (of *Gone with the Wind* [1939] fame), was also consulted on the script. Although his suggestions were ignored, Selznick brought with him stars such as Orson Welles, whose suggestion of a 'line of dialogue concerning Swiss cuckoo clocks' (Preface, *TM*, p. 4) famously was not. (Welles's line is itself a supreme piece of adaptation, a pithy reworking of the sentiment of an 1885 lecture by the American artist James McNeill Whistler [Drazin, 2000, pp. 75–6].) The concept of the novelist as isolated artist can be contested when we consider the influence, argument, advice and editorial intervention which determine the work of almost every modern author. In much the same way, the film of *The Third Man* is not the sole product of one author, but a collaborative project which began with Korda and Greene, and was developed by Greene and Reed, who together produced several 'treatments' based on the novella (Preface, *TM*, p. 4). Greene describes this division of labour in the Preface to the novella, and the dedication to Reed ('in memory of so many early morning Vienna hours at Maxim's, the Casanova, the Oriental') in particular underlines the collaborative, and occasionally convivial, nature of their creative process.

In addition, the success and effectiveness of the film was, and is, partly determined by the work of its cinematographer Robert Krasker (recipient of the film's only Academy Award); the assistant directing of Guy Hamilton (later the director of several Bond films); the film editing of Oswald Hafenrichter and the indigenous Viennese music of Anton Karas, which achieved phenomenal international success ('He'll have you in a dither with his zither', as publicity materials declared). Aside from its look and its sound, the film features some extraordinary performances across the full range of the cast list, including uncredited extras from the streets of Vienna and uncredited early appearances by actors who would go on to be more well known (such as Lee Strasberg, later the artistic director of the Actors Studio in 1951 and pioneer of Method Acting). The film also features cameos by well-known British actors such as Wilfrid Hyde-White and by well-established Austrian theatre and film actors who were little known elsewhere, including Ernst Deutsch, Paul Hoerbiger, Erich Ponto, Hedwig Bleibtreu and Siegfried Breuer, and, in the central roles, Trevor Howard, Bernard Lee, Alida Valli, Joseph Cotten and Orson Welles.

One of the key aspects of the film are the myths that continue to surround it. Greene was not necessarily even Korda's first choice of author to provide a film treatment, and the list of actors considered but not eventually cast in *The Third Man* has added to its folklore. High-profile Hollywood stars such as Cary Grant and James Stewart were considered for the role of Martins before Cotten was cast, as was Barbara Stanwyck for the role of Anna, played eventually by Valli. Renowned British actors such as Roger Livesey and Ralph Richardson were frontrunners to play Calloway before Howard was cast (Drazin, 2000, pp. 29–33), and an astonishingly diverse range of actors from both sides of the Atlantic – including Noël Coward, David Niven, Rex Harrison, Robert Taylor and Robert Mitchum – were considered as possible 'Harry Limes'. Yet despite all of these variables, the resulting film is an example of perfect casting. To take just Welles, Peter William Evans notes that Harry Lime is an embodiment of 'the most terrible of all outsider figures, Satan himself' (Evans, 2005, p. 98): Orson Welles, the maverick genius of cinema and *enfant terrible* who had spearheaded *Mercury Theatre on the Air*'s 'War of the Worlds' (1938) and provoked William Randolph Hearst with *Citizen Kane* (1941), was the ideal actor to play this charming devil of the post-war world. Intriguingly, the promotional materials for *The Third Man* play up Welles's divisive, Lime-like charm and force of will: 'An intense individualist, a restless experimentalist, an outspoken opinionist and critic, he is a man you can like or dislike, a man whose work you can admire or hate; but [...] none can ignore either Orson Welles or what he does' (BFI, 1949, p. 5). The same publicity materials also luridly claim that 'If there were 10,000 Orson Welles, society would fall apart like an exploding bomb' (BFI, 1949, p. 5); as well as catering to the myth of the artist as a destructive force, it is almost as if, in this supreme identification of the character and the actor playing him, Welles-as-Lime is himself somehow responsible for the bomb-damaged landscape of post-war Vienna.

That *The Third Man* was an immediate and abiding success partly explains why celebrants flock to the work to claim it as the stroke of genius of one person, usually at the expense of another. Greene, for one, attributed the success of the film to Reed and played down the role of Selznick, whom he saw as a rather ridiculous figure. This 'insider's view' of the production has since been redressed by critics such as Charles Drazin, who paints a more balanced picture of

The Third Man process (though he appears to be in agreement with Greene in describing Selznick as 'a conceited oaf' [Drazin, 2000, p. 118]). A fine example of another's 'laying claim' to *The Third Man* can be found in Orson Welles's account of the making of the film in an interview with the director Peter Bogdanovich:

Peter Bogdanovich: Besides playing Harry Lime, what else did you do on it?
Orson Welles: I wrote my part–
Peter Bogdanovich: Every word of it?
Orson Welles: Carol Reed is the kind of director who'll use any ideas – anything that's going. I had notions for the dialogue, and Carol liked them. Except for my rather minor contribution, the story, of course, was by the matchless Graham Greene. And the basic idea – though he took no credit for it – was Alex Korda's. (Welles and Bogdanovich, 1993, p. 220)

The implications of this account have been fiercely contested, not least by Drazin who debunks the hagiography of Welles's biographers Peter Cowie and Charles Higham, who like Welles downplay Reed's contribution (Drazin, 2000, pp. 78–81). As for Welles 'writing his part', it is a worthwhile enterprise to compare the prose and screen versions of the Big Wheel scene: although there are no cuckoo clocks in Greene's novella, both episodes contain equivalent or identical turns of phrase and the same overriding mood of suspense and chilling nihilism.

Given the film's collaborative aspect, it is perhaps inevitable that there are 'many differences between the story and the film', as Greene underlines in his Preface to the novella (Preface, *TM*, p. 4). Some of these differences are small and 'superficial' (Preface, *TM*, p. 4) and – aptly for a story set in a city divided between several different countries – concern issues of nationality. Martins and Lime, played by the American actors Joseph Cotton and Orson Welles (who had worked together on *Citizen Kane* [1941] and *The Magnificent Ambersons* [1942]), are now American rather than English, and the novella's references to their shared public-school background (a familiar trope in Greene) have been dropped. In addition, Martins's 'absurd Christian name', as the narrator terms it (*TM*, p. 10), was changed from 'Rollo' to the more American-sounding 'Holly', at Cotton's request (Cotton felt that 'Rollo' somehow connoted homosexuality, echoing Selznick's crudely expressed yet insightful belief that *The Third Man* contains a hidden 'queer' narrative involving Lime and Martins: 'It's just buggery, boys' [Cited in

Watts, 1997, p. 191].) That both lead characters were now American instead of English arguably made the film more marketable in the United States. For the same reason, the character of Colonel Cooler was made a Rumanian instead of an American because, as Greene notes, 'Mr Orson Welles' engagement [as Harry Lime] had already supplied us with one American villain' (Preface, *TM*, p. 4). Greene was apparently keen not to ruffle other national sensibilities, too: 'The episode of the Russians kidnapping Anna (a perfectly possible incident in Vienna) was eliminated', as 'it threatened to turn the film into a propaganda picture' (Preface, *TM*, p. 5) – though this, as James Sexton underlines, did not prevent the Russians from being 'angered over [Greene's] depiction of them' in the film (Sexton, 2005, p. xix). Anna's nationality, like that of Martins, Lime and Cooler, is also subtly modified: whereas in the novella she is a Hungarian, in the film she is of Czech origin. In each case, she hails from a country now under Soviet rule. As Cedric Watts points out, the film 'enlarged the role of Anna Schmidt'; it also 'added more action (in the form of chases) to the plot', 'and made Martins's reluctance to betray Lime more protracted' (Watts, 1997, p. 191).

Another minor change concerns what the narrator refers to as 'that absurd episode of the British Council lecturer' (*TM*, p. 7). In the novella this episode is both a *deus ex machina*, allowing the penniless Martins – on the cusp of leaving Vienna – to stay on in the city, and a comic interlude, setting up the lecture that Martins will give to an audience who think him to be his eminent namesake (his pen-name is 'Dexter'), even when – or rather because – he declares fellow pulp Western writer Zane Grey to be on a par with James Joyce, Virginia Woolf and Gertrude Stein: 'He didn't realize it, but he was making an enormous impression. Only a great writer could have taken so arrogant, so original a line' (*TM*, p. 56). This is why the narrator refers to the episode as 'absurd'. In the film, however, the absurdity lies elsewhere. When the lecture takes place (under the auspices of the fictional 'British Section for Cultural Re-Education' rather than the British Council), Martins is revealed to be wholly ignorant of his subject, 'The Contemporary Novel', and makes a fool of himself. This is more in keeping with the film's depiction of Martins as a blunderer who thinks he is in one of his own stories, with post-war Vienna (as we have seen) his modern-day Wild West. This self-identification is foregrounded during the lecture itself when, pressed for details of his forthcoming work, Martins claims to be writing a story called 'The Third Man' (*TM*, p. 55).

As with so many adaptations of Greene, from *Brighton Rock* (1947) to *The Quiet American* (1958), a much bigger alteration concerns the film's ending. The happy ending of the novella was replaced with a bleaker ending by Reed, who felt that the original was too artificially superficial. During the funeral scene at the end of the novella, Anna walks away from Lime's grave and past Martins, who catches her up, and the implication (one encouraged by the narrator's inference) is that he and Anna will begin a new life together: 'it was like the end of a story except that before they turned out of my sight her hand was through his arm – which is how a story usually begins' (*TM*, p. 98). In the film, however, Anna walks away from Lime's grave but also away from Martins in an apparent snub, and off into the middle distance as the credits roll. As such, one of the few happier endings to be found in Greene's fiction was transformed during the process of adaptation into an unhappy one, much to Greene's disappointment at the time, who claimed it represented '[o]ne of the very few major disputes between Carol Reed and myself' – though he concedes that Reed was subsequently 'proved triumphantly right' (Preface, *TM*, p. 4). In a significant sense, of course, the novella does contain an 'unhappy' ending, of sorts, one that concerns not the characters but the city of Vienna itself. The dispersal of snow and ice at the end of the story does not signify spring – and by extension, the possibility of renewal and reconstruction – but instead carries a characteristically Greeneian sense of gloom: 'all over Vienna the snow melted, and the ugly ruins came to light again: steel rods hanging like stalactites, and rusty girders thrusting like bones through the grey slush' (*TM*, p. 98).

Another major difference (which Greene does not mention) lies in the choice of narrator. The narrator in the novella is Major Calloway, whereas in the film it appears to be an unnamed black marketeer: 'We'd run anything, if people wanted it enough and had the money to pay.' This situates the narrator nearer the criminal world of Lime, and away from Calloway's world of police-work. Indeed, in the novella the narrative is itself a piece of police case-work, of sorts – 'reconstructed' from Calloway's 'own files' and eye-witness testimony (*TM*, p. 7). The cynical tone of Calloway's narration is retained, however, as is suggested by the film's scene-setting voice-over (spoken by an uncredited Reed), which repeats almost verbatim Calloway's opening description of Vienna: 'I never knew Vienna between the wars, and I am too young to remember the old Vienna with its Strauss music and its bogus easy charm; to me it is simply a city of undignified ruins which turned that February into great glaciers of snow and ice' (*TM*, p. 7).

Like the novella, the film contrasts the historic image of Vienna as a city rich in culture, music, art and science, with the post-war image of it as presented by the camera, showing bomb-damaged buildings, ruined churches, bodies floating in the Danube and rubble everywhere. Like the novella (and like Greene's other works about the war *The Ministry of Fear* [1943] and *The End of the Affair* [1951]), the film hereby offers 'a powerful commentary on [...] the indiscriminate havoc wreaked by modern warfare' (Watts, 1997, p. 191), in particular aerial warfare. This commentary is made all the more powerful for the use of actual footage of Vienna after the war, which gives this opening sequence a documentary feel – an 'air of being on the spot in the rubble of Vienna, 1949' (Coroneos, 2002, 159). (That said, the film was accused in some quarters of presenting only a partial view of the city by neglecting to show signs of post-war socio-economic recovery, which partly accounts for its initially cool reception in Austria [Coroneos, 2002, p. 161].) More importantly, however, the discrepancy between the traditional image of Vienna conjured by the voice-over and the post-war scene presented by the camera is dramatically heightened because these images – the one spoken, the other visualized by the camera – are presented simultaneously to the viewer.

Another powerful aspect of the film is its overall visual aesthetic. The black-and-white cinematography – shot by Robert Krasker, who had collaborated with Reed on another thriller about a hunted man, *Odd Man Out* (1947) – draws upon and extends the tropes and techniques of expressionist cinema and contemporary film noir. It had also long been the preferred medium of Greene, who felt that colour cinematography could not reproduce 'the suit that has been worn too long, [or] the oily hat' (*Pleasure-Dome*, p. 8), and that a monochrome palette better suited his fiction because it more closely conveyed the characteristically shabby textures of 'Greeneland'. (Indeed, Greene later mischievously claimed he saw 'the world in black and white, with an occasional touch of colour' [Allain, 1983, p. 134].) As if to underline Greene's exhortations elsewhere on the central importance in his works of 'point of view' (*A Sort of Life*, p. 144) – perhaps most notably in 'The Basement Room', where the narrative is focalized through a young boy – the film is also distinctive for its disorientating use of camera-angles. Cedric Watts describes 'the nervous shifts in camera-angles, now looking down from an immense height, now moving at gutter-level; now focusing microscopically on a telling detail of facial expression, now taking in a panorama of ruined buildings and empty streets' (Watts, 1997, p. 192). Krasker's black-and-white and often

strangely canted images won him and the film an Oscar. They were
not to all tastes, however. According to Reed, the American director
William Wyler reportedly sent him a spirit level along with a note
asking him to 'put it on the top of the camera' 'next time [he made] a
picture' (Samuels, 1972, p. 172). Meanwhile the *Observer*'s film critic
C. A. Lejeune, who earlier had praised the Boulting brothers' 1947
adaptation of Greene's *Brighton Rock*, bemoaned Reed's 'habit of
printing his scenes askew, with floors sloping at a diagonal and close-
ups deliriously tilted' (*Observer*, 4 September 1949, p. 6).

Yet *The Third Man* is also consciously drawing here upon and extending the techniques of expressionist cinema and film noir, where 'camera
work is as crucial an element as any' in establishing what Greene in
his Preface to the novella calls 'characterization [...] mood and atmosphere' (*TM*, p. 3), and where 'observational realism [is] constantly in
tension with the rendering of anguished inner states' (McFarlane,
2005, p. 393). In addition to these generic affiliations, the film's camera
angles – as if shot from the very craters left by the war – are integral to
capturing Greene and Reed's vision of the war-damaged topography of
Vienna, while also gesturing towards the skewed moral terrain of the
city after the war, where black marketeers and other dubious goings-on
were rife: there are many lingering shots of deserted streets, suggesting
'the scene of a crime' (Coroneos, 2002, p. 162). Equally, the 'look' of
the film also reflects *The Third Man*'s generic origins in the spy thriller
and the detective novel, as Coroneos has suggested:

> The extraordinary *mise-en-scène*, with its crazy angles, tilted frames, dead
> vistas, blind buildings, and so on, constantly draws attention to the fact
> that post-war Vienna is nothing but surveilled boundaries; it is a city of
> zones, passports, checkpoints, and military police [...] upon which the film
> focuses its aesthetic and technical interest. (Coroneos, 2002, p. 161)

The film's 'look' and the techniques used to generate this, in other
words, capture the sense of paranoia and mistrust which characterize
post-war Vienna, while also remaining true to the novella's generic
affiliations.

In addition, Greene's novella anticipates the visual realization of
certain key scenes in the film, most notably Lime's first appearance,
as Rob White underlines: '"a window curtain was drawn petulantly
back by some sleeper he had awakened, and the light fell straight
across the narrow street and lit up the features of Harry Lime."'
Likewise Lime's final moments, 'crawling towards a grille connecting
the sewers to the street: "he was in great pain and just as an animal

creeps into the dark to die, so I suppose a man makes for the light"'
(White, 2012c). In this regard, the novella anticipates the way the film
would be marketed and publicized: posters for it feature a man in one
of these underground waterways, the roof of the sewer providing a
natural 'frame' for the poster while also suggesting the man's entrapment. The novella is richly imbued not only with a sense of the visual,
but also of sound, and the characterization of Lime is again instruc-
tive on this point. Greene did not have Anton Karas's zither music in
mind when writing the treatment – this being a late, but inspired, decision during the shooting of the film. Yet in the treatment Lime does
have his own 'signature tune' (*TM*, p. 16), a piece of music he claims to
have composed (it is plagiarized, of course) and which he recurrently
whistles when he appears.

Greene later admitted a personal preference for his first collaboration with Reed, *The Fallen Idol*: he saw it as a 'writer's film', whereas
The Third Man is a director's film (Parkinson, 1993, p. 558). Yet in
a significant sense *The Third Man* is also a 'writerly' film. As Brian
Lindsay Thomson explains:

> Carol Reed's film of Greene's script did many of the things Greene's
> earlier novels had done: it mixed genres and constantly set the viewer at
> odds with the allegedly fixed rules of generic convention. It ended on an
> ambitious, half-comic and half-tragic note for its protagonist, and failed
> to deliver the tidy resolution that even progressive intellectuals associated
> with the medium in general and with Hollywood in particular. (Thomson,
> 2009, p. 85)

In other words, *The Third Man* changed the rules of generic cinema
just as Greene in the 'treatment' for the film had mixed together
different genres to create a work that was part Cold War 'thriller',
part romantic drama, part detective story (with Martins in the middle of his own modern 'whodunnit') and even part Western, producing something which as a whole appealed to popular and intellectual
audiences alike. This crossing of genres is reflected in early reviews
of the film, which variously label it a 'murder mystery' (*News of the
World*), a work of gothic 'terror and suspense' (*The People*), and –
recalling the dominant mode of Greene's novels from the previous
decade – a 'thriller' (*Sunday Chronicle*; *Evening News*). Moreover, as
Thomson argues, Greene and Reed 'succeeded in producing popular cinema that encouraged intellectuals to apprehend and formulate
its significance in literary terms' (Thomson, 2009, p. 83). To put it
another way, *The Third Man* is a pioneering example of cinema, an

adaptation which is as thoroughly crafted, and which should be 'read', as literature.

Exercises

- Compare the opening montage of the film of *The Third Man* with the opening chapter of Greene's novella. How do both pieces create a sense of place, history or contemporary political or cultural crisis?
- Analyse the formal style of the film (including its use of shadows, angles and music) in relation to Greene's narrative style (including description, voice and imagery).
- Greene creates a 'happy ending' for the novella, whereas the film ends on a very different note. Compare these endings closely, using this as a starting point to explore endings in other films (for instance, in genres such as the thriller, the western, film noir, or adventure films).
- Compare the Wiener Riesenrad (the 'Great Wheel') scene in the film and in Chapter 14 of the novella. How do both versions establish a sense of place and perspective? In addition, look at the dialogue in both versions and establish the similarities and the differences. Some critics and biographers have extolled Orson Welles's role in the film and in this scene in particular. Using Greene's novella as a starting point, explore the performance and interpretation of their respective roles by Joseph Cotton and Orson Welles in this scene.

The afterlife of *The Third Man*

The enormous popular and critical success of *The Third Man* led to a legacy of subsequent adaptation. On radio, the BBC aired several adaptations of *The Third Man* in the years following the release of the film, including one-hour versions in 1950 and 1959 and a full-length 90-minute production in 1971. On American radio, the *United States Steel Hour* featured Joseph Cotton reprising his screen role for a live audio adaptation of the film (January 1951), while the hugely popular *Lux Radio Theater* (a series which specialized in live audio versions of Hollywood films) presented two one-hour productions of *The Third Man*, first with Joseph Cotton (April 1951) and subsequently with Ray Milland as Holly Martins (February 1954).

In addition to these one-off audiophonic re-imaginings of *The Third Man*, the BBC also produced a radio drama series called *The Third Man: The Adventures of Harry Lime*, which aired some 52 half-hour episodes between 1951 and 1952. The series featured Orson Welles as Harry Lime and, on occasion, as scriptwriter, recalling his reputed similar involvement in Greene's original screenplay. As well as the distinctive voice of Welles, listeners also heard the familiar tones of the Anton Karas theme tune. The premise to the series is elucidated by its arresting opening monologue:

> Orson Welles: [GUNSHOT] That was the shot that killed Harry Lime. He died in a sewer in Vienna as those of you know who saw the movie *The Third Man*. Yes, that was the end of Harry Lime. But it was not the beginning. No, he had many lives. And I can tell you about all of them. How do I know? Because my name is Harry Lime.

As the series focuses on the adventures of Harry Lime, it is no surprise that he is less of a diabolical figure than in the film. The radio series makes Harry a hero, albeit an ambiguous and roguish one. As John Dunning explains:

> Lime's escapades took centre stage, his career as a prince of knaves coming into sharp focus. He was a double-dealing money-grubber who managed to remain sympathetic and at times almost admirable in his deceptions. Lime stole from the rich and gave to the poor, and Harry Lime was usually the poorest chap he knew. (Dunning, 1998, p. 663)

Dunning's description makes it clear that on the airwaves Lime becomes a kind of latter-day Robin Hood figure. All the same, the radio series consistently explores the 'dark' side of Lime. In one episode, 'The Third Woman' (December 1951), Lime is recruited – much to his own amusement – by British Intelligence to act as a double agent and help locate guided missiles being produced by Germany in wartime Europe (of the sort featured in Greene's *The End of the Affair*, published the same year). His commanding officer looks through Lime's dossier and states: 'if we could prove half of the stuff in this file you'd be celebrating your hundredth birthday in a military prison.' Later in the same episode, Harry endeavours to rescue a woman being held captive in the German embassy in Lisbon, and we see how Harry turns the tables and his subsequent interrogation technique:

Harry Lime:	Well … Well, Gerhardt, here we are…
Gerhardt:	Keep your hands up.
Harry Lime:	The ambassador says I'm stupid, Gerhardt, do you agree with him?

Gerhardt:	All the Americans are stupid.
Harry Lime:	Do you think it would be stupid for me to try and get that gun away from you, Gerhardt? Well, I suppose it would but anyway I'm going to try...! [SOUND OF STRUGGLE AND GUNSHOT]
Gerhardt:	Agh!
Harry Lime:	Sorry, I only got you in the leg, old man, but I never was much of a shot.
Gerhardt:	Please!
Harry Lime:	What I need ... what I need today is to practice my marksmanship and since this is such a nice sound proof room.
Gerhardt:	Ah! What are you doing!?
Harry Lime:	What shall I try for, Gerhardt, an arm or the other leg!?
Gerhardt:	No! No!
Harry Lime:	Alright then, where's the girl?
Gerhardt:	What girl? [GUNSHOT] Help!
Harry Lime:	That was the right hand wasn't it, Gerhard? Now then, let's try for a foot!
Gerhardt:	No! No! She's in there! Through that door!
Harry Lime:	Okay, thanks! [FOOTSTEPS AND DOOR OPENING] Julie! Julie!

Just as Orson Welles was perfectly cast as the original screen Harry Lime, he was adept at playing charismatic yet somewhat mischievous figures on air. In the late 1930s Welles had played the eponymous hero in the popular radio series *The Shadow*, a superhero with an intriguingly ambiguous side. In 1952, the same year as *The Third Man: The Adventures of Harry Lime*, Welles played Professor Moriarty in 'The Final Problem', an episode in the BBC radio series *The Adventures of Sherlock Holmes*, opposite John Gielgud (Holmes) and Ralph Richardson (Watson).

A few years after *The Third Man: The Adventures of Harry Lime* on radio, an Anglo-American syndicated show would once again create a series around Harry Lime with *The Third Man* (1959–65), a very successful television series which featured almost eighty 30-minute dramas. The series used the Anton Karas theme tune, but the lead role was played by Michael Rennie, whose Lime was now a wealthy art dealer and conman with, essentially, a heart of gold. The journey towards a more Robin Hood-like figure, inaugurated in the BBC radio Harry Lime, was now complete.

The fascinating legacy to Greene's demonic Harry Lime, murdered with such finality at the end of the original *Third Man*, bears testament to the success of the film and the power and afterlife of Greene's construction. The character of Harry Lime – more than Holly Martins or any of the other main characters – evidently fascinated radio and television audiences in the 1950s and early 1960s, and the audience's love of the original film, its theme tune and Orson Welles's performance no doubt fuelled a desire for 'earlier' Harry Lime adventures. In the process of inventing all-new storylines of the days before post-war Vienna, these versions underscore the creative possibilities of the prequel as an adaptive resource.

Exercises

- Locate a radio adaptation of *The Third Man* and compare it with the original film. What is the same? What is different? Is anything added or removed?
- Locate some examples of the radio or television dramas mentioned in this chapter that flesh-out Lime's backstory before his demise in Vienna. Analyse how the figure of Harry Lime has been changed and what remains similar. In addition, examine how a social or political context is created around Harry Lime and compare this to the creation of post-war Austria in the original film of *The Third Man*.
- Compare Harry Lime with other anti-heroes in popular culture that have been reworked and re-imagined: for example, how does the re-adaptation of Harry Lime compare with Dracula, Batman, various Bond villains, Patricia Highsmith's Tom Ripley, and so on?

Our Man in Havana

Greene's 1958 novel *Our Man in Havana* is set in pre-revolutionary Cuba. It depicts the Cuban capital as a seedy and corrupt place, where people are tortured and murdered by the secret police, represented here by the sinister Captain Segura (based on the real head of President Batista's secret police, Captain Ventura). The plot centres on the strangely named figure of Wormold, a divorced vacuum cleaner salesman, who ekes out a financially cramped existence in Havana with his daughter Milly. He is recruited as an agent by British Intelligence and, sensing an opportunity to help provide for Milly's increasingly extravagant lifestyle, responds by employing a network of imaginary informants and collecting their pay. He then begins sending fictitious reports to his superiors in London, including one containing plans of a Cuban secret weapon based on one of his hoovers. Things get serious, however, when his reports are considered real by rival agents, who attempt to assassinate his imaginary spies and, in a key scene, Wormold himself. He kills his would-be assassin Carter and is recalled to London, where his deception – of potentially enormous embarrassment to his employers – is suppressed. Rather than being punished, Wormold is instead rewarded with a position lecturing new agents on espionage. Despite the seriousness of its backdrop and some of its themes, the novel – a satire of Greene's former employers in the Secret Intelligence Service (SIS; later MI6) – is also expressly an 'entertainment', and certainly one of his lighter and more comedic works. It remains, as one early reviewer put it, 'as comical, satirical, atmospheric an "entertainment" as he has given us' (Cited in Watts, 1997, p. 66). Along with its slight precursor *Loser Takes All* (1955), it is also one of his few novels with an unambiguously happy ending.

The inspirations of *Our Man in Havana* are partly to be found in two films from the mid-1930s: William Wyler's *These Three* (1936), which like *Our Man* is about a lie which gets disastrously out of hand (Sinyard, 2003, p. 55), and Pierre Billon's *Deuxième bureau* (1936), about which Greene wrote at the time: 'what an amusing film of the Secret Service could be made if the intention was satiric and not romantic, the treatment realistic' (*Pleasure-Dome*, p. 47). Another of the main inspirations for the novel, of course, lay in Greene's own experiences as a British Intelligence operative, during not the Cold War but the Second World War. He was recruited by his sister Elisabeth in 1941, and was sent to Sierra Leone (then a British protectorate) in West Africa. Though 'a lonely, out-of-the-way posting' (R. Greene, 2007, p. xxv), far removed from the comparative glamour of the Cuba of *Our Man in Havana*, the method of Greene's recruitment is not so far removed from the spying-as-family-affair of *Our Man*. It was while in Sierra Leone that he wrote the London-set espionage thriller *The Ministry of Fear* (1943), which was immediately filmed by Fritz Lang in 1944. Greene's experiences in Sierra Leone were later fictionalized in his novel of wartime British expatriate life, *The Heart of the Matter* (1948), and this was also swiftly adapted for the screen. Greene's spy years in Africa were therefore a fruitful source for his fiction and for films of his fiction. His activities in Africa – 'run[ing] agents into the Vichy colonies' (*Ways of Escape*, p. 238) – also recall some of the war-films of the period, in particular Michael Curtiz's *Casablanca* (1942), but for one genre-defying detail: these activities were, by his own admission, fruitless and 'futile' (*WE*, p. 238). Greene then moved to another section of counter-espionage, this time monitoring the activities of German Abwehr agents in Portugal, and it was during this period that the central conceit of *Our Man in Havana* began to take shape when he turned up several cases of agents fabricating reports – including a double-agent named 'Garbo', after the world-famous film actress Greta Garbo. In *Ways of Escape*, Greene recalls 'how easily in Africa I could have played a similar game': 'nothing pleased the services at home more than the addition of a card to their intelligence files', and there 'was no rival organization in the field [...] with whose reports mine could be compared' (*WE*, p. 239). Notwithstanding its seeming outlandishness, therefore, *Our Man in Havana* at one level *is* the 'realistic' treatment that Greene envisaged before the war in his review of Billon's spy drama.

Wormold is said to keep a cache of flammable celluloid sheets 'ready for a final conflagration' (*Our Man in Havana*, p. 110) should he need to destroy any incriminating papers, and this intriguing use of film for destructive ends offers a reminder that Greene's spy story has cinematic beginnings. Greene had originally developed the story for the Brazilian director Alberto Cavalcanti during the 1940s. Cavalcanti had directed *Went the Day Well?* (1942), an adaptation of Greene's short tale about a German invasion of an English village during the Second World War, 'The Lieutenant Died Last' (1940), and had asked Greene 'to write a[nother] film for him' (*WE*, p. 238). Like *Our Man in Havana*, 'The Lieutenant Died Last' focuses on the nebulous but real threat of a foreign enemy (here fascist Germany rather than communist Russia), and was in turn a modern re-casting of the late-Victorian invasion novels of Erskine Childers and William Le Queux. In fact, the first version of *Our Man in Havana* (provisionally entitled *Nobody to Blame*) also featured Germany as a foe, and was not set in Havana at all, but in late 1930s Tallinn, Estonia. Greene began to have doubts, however, when it occurred to him that 'the reader could feel no sympathy for a man who was cheating his country in Hitler's day' (*WE*, p. 241). Sensing that a film which poked fun at British Intelligence might, during a time of war, likewise be something of a hostage to fortune, Cavalcanti's interest also waned. The story was put on hold until, having visited Cuba several times in the 1950s, Greene felt he had found in Havana an appropriately licentious setting, and in the Cold War a conflict that was, unlike the Second World War, appropriately absurd: 'for who can accept the survival of Western capitalism as a great cause?' (*WE*, p. 241). This moving of the action from pre-war Estonia to the Cuba of the recent past is also in keeping with the vaguely colonial settings and themes of his fiction of the time: *The Quiet American* (1955) was set in Vietnam during the collapse of French rule, and his next novel, *A Burnt-Out Case* (1961), would be set in the central Africa of Conrad's *Heart of Darkness* (1899) during the last days of the Belgian Congo. Greene's fiction was becoming increasingly concerned with the role of the colonial, ex-colonial and neo-colonial world, the proxy settings where the 'hot' battles of the Cold War would be played out over the coming years.

Malcolm Muggeridge, a former spy like Greene, praised the novel as 'the most brilliant book of intelligence that's ever been written because it gets inside the whole fantasy [of spying]' (Cited in Sherry, 2005, p. 106). Indeed, many of the novel's seemingly far-fetched elements, as with Greene's putting of the 'Garbo' episode to fictional use, are drawn from real-life. Wormold's friend Hasselbacher, for instance, was based on a German acquaintance of Greene's who, like his fictional counterpart in *Our Man in Havana*, had seen service in the German army during the First World War and was known to dress up in full uniform on important occasions (*WE*, p. 250). Other elements drawn from real-life include Greene's reputedly modelling *Our Man*'s Chief of Intelligence on the former head of SIS Sir Stuart Menzies (Watts, 1997, p. 65), while Greene's code number from his SIS days, 59200, also features in the novel (Shelden, 1994, p. 33). Wormold's foe Carter, meanwhile, draws on Greene's memories of his nemesis from his days as a schoolboy in Berkhamsted, as described in *A Sort of Life* (1971); Wormold's killing of Carter, then, represents another vicarious victory for Greene (the name recurs in the short stories 'The Blue Film' [1954] and 'Mortmain' [1967]). Wormold, however, has according to Greene 'no origin that I can recognise' (*WE*, p. 250) – which, for a character who invents figures from thin air – is nothing if not apt. Wormold's creation of an imaginary body of agents could be taken as an allegory of artistic and even literary creativity (Sinyard, 2003, p. 67). Yet Wormold's creativity is itself, in a sense, also a recycling of a familiar theme of Greene's: like his earlier works 'The Basement Room' or *The Quiet American*, or his next novel *A Burnt-Out Case*, the actions of an apparent innocent prove deadly. Cedric Watts points out that, 'though it mocks the rhetoric of the Cold War, *Our Man in Havana* does not purport to be making any probing analysis of international relations' (Watts, 1997, p. 66). At the same time, however, much like its hero Wormold the novel stumbles onto a greater political truth, and its depiction of Western unease over secret weapons on the island of Cuba could be seen to anticipate the Cuban Missile Crisis of 1962. Like *The Quiet American*, which anticipates the growing and disastrous military presence of the United States in Vietnam, *Our Man in Havana*, for all its apparent fancifulness, might instead be regarded as a work of significant, if accidental, political foresight.

Our Man in Havana was generally well received on its publication in October 1958, both at home and abroad. That a Soviet cosmonaut reportedly took the novel with him into space to read (Sherry, 2005, p. 747) further attested to Greene's soaring international popularity and reputation. According to Norman Sherry, the novel attracted attention from film companies interested in adapting it several months before it was even published (Sherry, 2005, p. 103). One name attached to the film was that of Alfred Hitchcock. Greene had met Hitchcock in 1936, shortly after the director had finished work on adapting another spy novel for the screen, Joseph Conrad's *The Secret Agent* (as *Sabotage*). The impression, however, was not a good one: 'I shuddered at the things he told me he was doing to Conrad's *Secret Agent*' (R. Greene, 2007, p. 79). This impression was also a lasting one: despite Hitchcock offering a reported £50,000 for the film rights (Falk, 2000, p. 101), Greene blocked the deal, feeling 'the book just wouldn't survive his touch' (Cited in Falk, 2000, p. 101). Carol Reed, with whom Greene had already collaborated to great acclaim on *The Fallen Idol* and *The Third Man*, was signed up to direct instead, with Greene again providing the screenplay, and a stellar cast that included Alec Guinness (as Wormold), Maureen O'Hara (as his fellow agent and love interest Beatrice), Ernie Kovacs (as the secret police chief Segura) and Noël Coward (as the spy recruiter Hawthorne). As with their most recent collaboration *The Third Man*, filming for which was split between Shepperton Studios, London and Vienna, the film would be shot largely on location.

This decision to shoot in Havana, however, proved one of the main obstacles in filming the novel. The political landscape of Cuba described in *Our Man in Havana* had shifted considerably since its publication, presenting Reed and Greene with a series of logistical problems. As Quentin Falk explains: 'The book was published in the last days of the Batista regime', but by 'the time the cast and crew descended on Havana six months later, the Castro revolt had succeeded.' How then, 'to keep Castro's bearded followers out of crowd scenes'? How to make 'extras wear the hated blue uniform of the Batista police'? And – above all – how to get the new government's 'seal of approval on the 30,000-word script' (Falk, 2000, pp. 102–3)?

The Castro government was keenly protective of the image it was trying to cultivate of the new Cuba, and was sensitive to the possibility that the film, with its allusions to the state-sponsored torture and killings that happened under Batista, might be misunderstood.

To get around this, the film opens with a caption that sets events firmly in the past, 'before the recent revolution'. The film then follows the source text more or less closely, the incongruous Americanization of Wormold's daughter aside, with main additions being of an expositional nature or to enlarge upon existing elements of the story. For instance, when Wormold's list of imaginary agents is received by London, Reed shows these enlistments being recruited, playfully leaving it to the audience to decide whether this re-enactment is taking place in Wormold's head or in the heads of his employers, who – as the novel underlines – are only too ready to buy into the fantasy themselves: 'The small shop for vacuum cleaners had been drowned beyond recovery in the tide of the Chief's literary imagination. Agent 59200/5 was established' (*OMH*, p. 46). Another slight enhancement concerns the film's ending. Having discovered Wormold's duplicity, his chiefs contrive to keep this a secret and away from the public. The camera then cuts to Wormold, Beatrice and Milly walking past a street vendor selling motorized toys, which bear an uncanny resemblance to the structures outlined in Wormold's fake plans. The ending hereby seems to offer a final, cutting comment on Greene's former employers as an organization that trades in secrets, but cannot seem to keep them.

Our Man in Havana was the last film on which Greene and Reed collaborated, marking the professional end of a relationship that stretched back to when Greene reviewed Reed's second film as a director, *Midshipman Easy*, for the *Spectator* in 1935. However, what would prove to be their swansong was never fully on song, and most critics are in agreement that their final collaboration is also a flawed one – and even a failure when measured against the lasting acclaim of *The Third Man*. On its release in 1960, although Coward's performance attracted some praise the film itself received largely indifferent reviews. To begin with, the film was hampered by problems of casting. In addition to the rather wooden Jo Morrow as Milly (whose performance Greene felt 'ruined' the film [Cited in Falk, 2000, p. 107]), such problems arguably ran to Reed himself, whose directorial talents were more suited to the noir of *The Fallen Idol* and *The Third Man* than the gentle comedy of *Our Man*. Indeed, as Neil Sinyard observes, *Our Man in Havana* would have been better suited as an

Ealing comedy, had Ealing not ceased production the same year the novel appeared (Sinyard, 2003, p. 68) – a point further underlined by the fact that its main star, Guinness, had starred in a string of Ealing films, most recently *The Ladykillers* (1955). The novel was also the unlikely basis of an opera of the same name in 1963, which like the film fared poorly with the critics: 'some people were very unkind to it', as Greene later reflected (*Sunday Times*, 5 March 1978, p. 37). The failure of *Our Man in Havana* also anticipated, and perhaps lay some of the ground for, a creatively fallow period for Greene. He had come to believe that his forthcoming novel *A Burnt-Out Case* not only marked, as its title suggests, something of a creative ebb, but would also probably be his last work as a novelist. Other novels would follow, yet at the time it seemed to Greene that his imagination, unlike Wormold's, had run dry.

Exercises

- Compare the novel *Our Man in Havana* to other espionage fiction by Greene such as *The Human Factor* (1978). What differences are there across these works in Greene's treatment of the subject? To what extent does the latter work adapt elements of the former?
- How does the film version of *Our Man in Havana* compare with other cinematic examples of the genre? Consider, for example, the James Bond movie franchise, or 'Cold War' novels by writers such as John le Carré or Len Deighton and the film, television and radio adaptations of these.
- Consider the place of satire and comedy in Greene's *Our Man in Havana*. How does Greene construct this? And how this has been translated onto the screen?

Chapter Three

Brighton Rock

Critically acclaimed on its publication in 1938, and popular with general readers ever since (Watts, 1997, pp. 40–1), *Brighton Rock* is arguably Greene's most well-known work of fiction. The novel has been part of school curricula in Britain for decades, and remains many readers' first point of entry into the canon of Greene's works. As we saw in Chapter One, it first appeared as a 'novel' in the United Kingdom but as an 'entertainment' in the United States. Yet this apparent generic contradiction does, in fact, reveal something essential about *Brighton Rock*. In this novel, Greene succeeds in combining aspects of popular genre in terms of plot and structure with literary technique in terms of style, a blend of 'high' and 'low' that led the American critic Morton D. Zabel to identify Greene as 'the [W. H.] Auden of the modern thriller' (Zabel, 1948, p. 273). In addition, this ability to straddle genres in turn reveals something essential about the reasons behind Greene's wide-ranging appeal, and why readers and adapters keep returning to his works.

From its memorably urgent opening sentence, *Brighton Rock* is a classic example of the thriller genre: 'Hale knew, before he had been in Brighton three hours, that they meant to murder him' (*Brighton Rock*, p. 3). However, unlike Greene's other 1930s thrillers such as *Stamboul Train* and *A Gun for Sale* (in which the murdered gangland figure Kite also appears), *Brighton Rock* is, like his subsequent novel *The Power and the Glory* (1940), also a work of significant literary ambition, and the first serious exploration in his fiction of the nature of evil, sin and religion. As if to underline its hybrid mixture of thriller and morality tale, its opening sentence sits next to an epigraph taken from the Jacobean tragedy *The Witch of Edmonton* (1621), by William Rowley, Thomas Dekker and John Ford: 'This were a fine reign:/To do ill and not hear of it again.' The novel's translation to the screen almost a decade later, for which Greene wrote the screenplay (his first adaptation of one of his own works), also initiated a remarkable sequence of successful adaptations of Greene's work: *Brighton Rock* (John Boulting, 1947), *The Fallen Idol* (Carol Reed, 1948) and *The Third Man* (Carol Reed, 1949). A second adaptation for the screen by Rowan Joffe (2010) some sixty years after the first – the third occasion in recent years that a major Greene novel has been adapted for the screen for a second time following Neil Jordan's *The End of the Affair* (1999) and Phillip Noyce's *The Quiet American* (2002) – testifies to the lasting pull of Greene's story on filmmakers and audiences alike.

The novel took shape during a transitional moment in Greene's career. He was arguably as much a travel writer as a novelist, having just published *Journey Without Maps* (1936), based on his visit in 1935 to Liberia in West Africa, and *The Lawless Roads* (1939), his travelogue about the religious purges in Mexico which later formed the basis of *The Power and the Glory* (1940), both of which remain classics of the genre. Greene's early novels, meanwhile, were expressly 'entertainments', aimed at (if not always able to secure) a popular audience. *Brighton Rock*, however, was Greene's first 'serious' novel. It marked a new direction for his fiction not just in terms of its more literary approach but also in terms of its commercial appeal: in his ten years as a novelist sales of his works (*Stamboul Train* aside) had remained small, and when *Brighton Rock* appeared he was finally lifted out of debt to his publishers Heinemann for the advances received for his early novels (*Ways of Escape*, p. 78). Although he was in his mid-thirties when it was published, *Brighton Rock* marked Greene's coming of age as a writer. In it, he 'had attained what most writers would desire: a style memorably distinctive and even idiosyncratic' (Watts, 1997, p. 159).

The novel also saw Greene honing his literary craft through his growing interest in and experience of cinema. He had recently been appointed the film critic for the *Spectator*, and was writing on film for another magazine, *Night and Day* (which he co-founded). It was during this period that he wrote the first of his film treatments for the producer Alexander Korda, *The Green Cockatoo* (William Cameron Menzies, 1937), which, like *Brighton Rock*, was about the world of homicidal racetrack gangs (Adamson, 1984, pp. 27–8), and this underlines the creative cross-fertilization between Greene's writing for the screen and his fiction. *Brighton Rock* would also draw on Greene's cinema-going more generally. Pinkie's tormentor, Ida Arnold, was partly modelled on the similarly formidable Mae West, in particular her racy 'Diamond Lil' incarnation (she is tellingly referred to as 'Lily' by her fellow pub-goers [*BR*, p. 5]). Meanwhile Pinkie himself seems to have been based partly on Joseph Conrad's 'Mr Jones', the cruelly misogynistic, possibly homosexual villain of Conrad's 1915 novel *Victory* (which Greene in 1937 had labelled one 'of the great English novels of the last fifty years' [*Collected Essays*, p. 139]), and partly on Humphrey Bogart's 'Baby-Face Martin' from William Wyler's 1937 film *Dead End* (Sinyard, 2003, p. 87), whose background of urban squalor and decay also chimes with Greene's vision of pre-war England in *Brighton Rock*: 'the houses which looked as if they had passed through an intensive bombardment, flapping gutters and glassless windows [...] the smashed and wasted ground in front where houses had been pulled down for model flats which had never gone up' (*BR*, p. 95). Another gangster picture, Julien Duvivier's *Pépé le Moko* (1937), was also 'a particular influence' on Greene during this period (Sinyard, 2003, p. 53). In fact, the novel's cinematic origins go back further than this, with Greene's cinema-going actually having begun *in* Brighton: this is where he saw his first film, an adaptation of Anthony Hope's *Sophy of Kravonia*, in 1911 (*WE*, p. 79).

Brighton Rock is set in a narrative present that is soon to become part of the past. As Greene later remarked, the novel drew on a background that was already passing into social history: '[the slum] Nelson Place has been cleared away since the war, and the Brighton race gangs were to all intents quashed for ever as a serious menace at Lewes Assizes a little before the date of my novel' (*WE*, p. 77). Similarly, a disclaimer at the beginning of the Boulting brothers' 1947 film of the novel announces that the Brighton it depicts – a place 'of dark alleyways and festering slums [...] crime and violence and gang warfare' – is 'now happily no more'. Although both the book and the film are explicitly set before the Second World War, both speak to the rise of gangsterism and racketeering in the years after the war – a theme of other British films from the period such as *They Made Me a Fugitive* (Alberto Cavalcanti, 1947) and *It Always Rains on Sundays* (Robert Hamer, 1947). In this way, the novel can be seen as not just having anticipated, but also as having helped to define, a particular brand of post-war English film noir.

Beyond this, *Brighton Rock* also left a significant and sizeable impression on the landscape of post-war fiction and film. Pinkie can be seen as a precursor to the equally disturbing and disturbed figure of Alex in Anthony Burgess's 1962 novel *A Clockwork Orange*, the source of Stanley Kubrick's notorious 1971 film adaption (Burgess's preceding novel *Devil of a State* [1961] was dedicated to Greene) and even of later American icons of juvenile delinquency such as Marlon Brando and James Dean. The novel casts a suspicious eye on the rise of popular culture, and this lends itself to Rowan Joffe's 2010 film version of *Brighton Rock*, with its cast of clashing Mods and Rockers in early 1960s Brighton. The razor gangs of Greene's novel also presage more recent adaptations such as the BBC television drama *Peaky Blinders* (2013–), Stephen Knight's re-imagining of a similarly murky and crime-ridden interwar England. In fact, the abiding influence of *Brighton Rock* can be felt on an abundance of classic and popular British crime dramas that have appeared since, from Mike Hodge's *Get Carter* (1971) to John Mackenzie's *The Long Good Friday* (1980), to Guy Ritchie's *Lock, Stock and Two Smoking Barrels* (1998): these are films which, despite their almost Jacobean levels of violence and retribution, can also be seen to be underpinned by a certain skewed morality. Other films falling into this bracket might include Paul McGuigan's *Gangster Number One* (2000), whose coldly murderous and ladder-climbing main character could almost be a grown-up facsimile of Pinkie, and Paul Andrew Williams's remarkable *London to Brighton* (2006), which likewise features a young girl in mortal peril from a local mobster and an older, damaged woman who tries to save her. All of these iterations of the British gangster film over the years can arguably be traced back to and grounded in Greene's novel.

The novel begins with a scene-setting depiction of a Whitsun holiday in Brighton which, in its rapid, montage-like interchange of imagery, seems ready-made for screen adaptation:

> They came in by train from Victoria every five minutes, rocked down Queen's Road standing on the tops of the little local trams, stepped off in bewildered multitudes into fresh and glittering air: the new silver paint sparkled on the piers, the cream houses ran away into the west like a pale Victorian water-colour; a race in miniature motors, a band playing, flower gardens in bloom below the front, an aeroplane advertising something for the health in pale vanishing clouds across the sky. (*BR*, p. 3)

Seemingly alone among this Whitsun holiday crowd is the figure of Hale. Hale is a journalist, in Brighton for the day in the guise of 'Kolley Kibber' for a competition run by his employer the *Daily Messenger*: his job is to deposit cards around the town, a large prize awaiting whoever confronts 'Kolley Kibber' and claims their reward, 'in the proper form of words and with a copy of the *Messenger* in his hand' (*BR*, p. 4). This gimmick of newspaper promotion was popular during the 1930s, most famously the *News Chronicle*'s character of 'Lobby Lud' (whose name Hale's alliterative pseudonym seems to conflate with that of the eighteenth-century poet and playwright Colley Cibber, immortalized in Alexander Pope's *The Dunciad*), and would have been immediately recognizable to the novel's contemporary audience.

This promotion is also an ingenious device for the construction of a familiar trope of Greene's early fiction, from *The Man Within* (1929), *Stamboul Train* (1932) and *A Gun For Sale* (1936), to *The Confidential Agent* (1939) and *The Power and the Glory* (1940): the 'man on the run'. As part of his job, Hale needs to adhere to a strict timetable which dictates where he needs to be at any given hour, and just as an eagle-eyed newspaper reader might apprehend Hale/'Kolley Kibber' and claim their ten guinea prize (a considerable sum of money in today's terms), so, too, might the members of a particular extortion gang, who are determined to apprehend him in the name of revenge. This is because Hale has somehow been involved in the murder of Kite, their former leader. The gang is now led by the disarmingly young 'Boy' called Pinkie, who wants Hale's blood. Hale's name therefore carries with it the suggestion of someone dragged or drawn forcibly, as befits his 'hunted man' status. It also belies his end: though suggestive of rude health (as in 'hale and hearty'), when confronted by the gang he dies of an apparent heart attack.

From its urgent opening sentence the chapter builds in suspense, matching the increasing anxiety of Hale as, alone in the heaving crowds of day-trippers ('Nobody paid any attention to Hale; no one seemed to be carrying a *Messenger*' [*BR*, p. 4]), and having realized his predicament, he desperately tries to stay alive. Hale's mounting desperation is sparingly revealed through telling visual clues such as the 'bitten nails' on his 'inky fingers' (p. 3), or the sudden 'slopping' of gin 'out of Hale's glass on to the bar' (p. 5) on hearing the voice of his nemesis, Pinkie, behind him. Hale attempts to befriend strangers in the belief that the gang 'hadn't the nerve to kill him in broad day before witnesses' (p. 7), and manages to latch on to the mature day-tripper Ida Arnold, who, like Pinkie, is introduced to the narrative (and to the reader) aurally, as a voice in the pub. This again bears the trace of the influence of cinema on Greene's literary craft: it was during roughly this period when, as a film critic for the *Spectator*, he became aware of the soundscape of cinema and the narrative power of '*selected* sounds' (*WE*, p. 39; emphasis in original). The song that Hale overhears Ida singing is 'She Wore a Wreath of Roses' by the Victorian poet Thomas Haynes Bayley, about the haunting of a widow by her old flame; this adds to his sense of desperation and thickens our sense of his plight, by invoking the hereafter to which the gang, and Pinkie in particular, plan to send him. Ida is a suggestively maternal figure, in whom Hale finds an unlikely saviour, and this is again registered sensorially: 'She smelt of soap and wine: comfort and peace and a slow sleepy physical enjoyment, a touch of the nursery and the mother, stole from the big tipsy mouth [...] and reached Hale's withered and frightened and bitter little brain' (*BR*, p. 14).

Hale escapes the confines of the pub, where Pinkie's gang might attack him unnoticed, to the seemingly safer crowds on the seafront. The narrative here switches from the external description of what Hale looks like to these crowds – 'the bony legs and the pigeon breast' – to inhabiting his point of view to present how the crowd appears to him: 'He couldn't see beyond the man in flannels just in front, and when he turned his vision was blocked by a brilliant scarlet blouse' (*BR*, pp. 11, 9). This sense of spatial confinement and entrapment is underlined by a corresponding sense of urgency and time: time is running out for Hale, just as his physical opportunities for escape are. He again meets Ida, who having warmed to his aura of pathos and desperation, takes him under her wing. However, she is startled when she leaves him for no more than 'four minutes' (*BR*, p. 18) and returns to find that her new friend has disappeared. This also comes as a shock to the reader: the early part of the narrative has been focalized through a character that, we are suddenly made to realize, is not in fact the focus of the story.

Hale's existence is a telescoped one in terms of time: he arrives in Brighton to begin his programme at ten o'clock (*BR*, p. 3), and his disappearance is marked by 'a clock away in the town [striking] half-past one' (p. 19). Hale's hour-by-hour timetable becomes Ida's few minutes in the ladies' lavatory, which in turn becomes his sudden, mysterious, yet absolute, termination. The seller of cheap wristwatches on the pier after Hale's disappearance suggestively drives this home: Hale is someone for whom time has run out. This was already suggested to us when we are told of Hale's circuit: 'yesterday Southend, today Brighton, tomorrow –' (p. 4). There is no tomorrow for 'Fred' Hale.

Nor is there any sense that he is bound, having later been cremated, for eternity: 'Fred dropped in indistinguishable grey ash on the pink blossoms: he became part of the smoke nuisance over London' (p. 35). Indeed, time is an important aspect of the narrative as a whole, which as a thriller is carefully and deliberately paced in terms of its plot sequence, and whose denouement – in line with its metaphysical ambitions – 'depends on coincidental meetings, lucky timings and unlikely sightings' (Watts, 1997, p. 178). Greene was keen that the screen adaptation of the novel would capture the sense of time of the original. In a 1946 letter to John Boulting, who would direct the first film of the novel (with his brother Roy Boulting as producer), Greene sets out precisely how he thinks it should open: with 'a succession of close-ups', much like the novel, of 'curtains being raised or shutters drawn back in the shops: the day's newspaper poster featuring Kolley Kibber being squeezed under the wire framework of a poster board: the fun cars on the pier being polished. [...] I express this very roughly and loosely but perhaps you will see the kind of tempo I feel the film should begin on' (R. Greene, 2007, p. 136).

As well as the visual descriptions and the sense of time, the cinematic is also inherent in sequences such as the pub scene in which Pinkie confronts Hale:

> "Look, take this *Messenger*. Read what it says there. You can have the whole prize. Ten guineas", he said. "You'll only have to send this form to the *Messenger*."
>
> "Then they don't trust you with the cash", the boy said, and in the other bar Lily began to sing, "We met – 'twas in a crowd – and I thought he would shun me." "Christ", the boy said, "won't anybody stop that buer's mouth?"
>
> "I'll give you a fiver", Hale said. "It's all I've got on me. That and my ticket."
>
> "You won't want your ticket", the boy said.
>
> "I wore my bridal robe, and I rivall'd its whiteness."
>
> The boy rose furiously, and giving way to a little vicious spurt of hatred – at the song? at the man? – he dropped his empty glass on to the floor. "The gentleman'll pay", he said to the barman and swung through the door of the private lounge. It was then Hale realized that they meant to murder him. (*BR*, pp. 6–7)

Again, the scene captures an enveloping sense of sound. However, rather than the presentation of 'selected sounds', here there is an overlapping, montage-like presentation of dialogue and sounds: the conversation between the increasingly apprehensive Hale and his tormenter Pinkie, the song from the other bar which threatens to drown out their conversation and the smashing of glassware which ends it. In his violent speech (his hatred of 'that buer' – a derogatory term for a woman) and actions (his deliberate smashing of the glass), Pinkie conveys a sense of menace; yet there are also levels of cool objectivity and uncertainty: although Pinkie moves 'furiously' and Hale must be in a state of building anxiety, the dialogue is 'said' by the characters rather than expressed via other, less neutral verbs of utterance. Finally, the narrative leaves it unclear as to whether Pinkie hates the song or Hale, the confusion over the action chiming with the represented confusion of sounds. The result of this approach is particularly cinematic, and typical of the objective, 'camera eye' method with which Greene's fiction was becoming associated (as one reviewer put it, 'It is the most filmically written book of Britain's most filmic writer' [*News Chronicle*, 10 January 1948. Cited in Falk, 2000, p. 49]). The sound and location is clearly presented and yet the interpretation of the characters is as ambiguous as it would be to a spectator watching a living character: we cannot 'see inside' them; rather, we see their surface actions and it is up to us to interpret these actions. It is only in the last line of the extract that we are given access to Hale's thoughts, as the meaning of Pinkie's remark about his now-superfluous ticket sinks in and he finally comprehends his peril.

Greene's depiction of Brighton itself is important here. Like the Nottwich of his preceding novel *A Gun For Sale* (a thinly veiled version of the Nottingham where he was apprenticed as a journalist), or the Southern England of his subsequent novel *The Confidential Agent*, Greene's Brighton is never merely part of the background. On the one hand, the town is realistically and accurately evoked, recalling the topographical exactness of the London of Charles Dickens or the Dublin of James Joyce's *Ulysses* (1922). Brighton had a particular grandeur during the Regency period of the 1810s (most clearly encapsulated in the Royal Pavilion, which figures in Neil Jordan's 1999 adaptation of Greene's *The End of the Affair*), and although it had lost some of this sheen it remained one of the pre-eminent English seaside resorts during the 1930s, thanks to an improvement in transport links and a rise in leisure time among the urban working class, which had made it easier for the crowds depicted in the novel to make the day-trip to 'London-by-the-Sea' (Feigel and Harris, 2009, p. 17, p. 29). Greene's Brighton is sociologically interesting for its description of the town's urban layout and local economy (Brighton is a place of urban decay and yet also tourist attraction), its sense of demographic, its use of the spoken language of the era (notably slang terms such

as 'buer' ['loose' woman], 'polony' [plump person], 'bogies' [police])
and its depiction of the criminal underworld of interwar Britain. This
is certainly a different Brighton to the cheery, carefree town that
features in Greene's *Travels With My Aunt* (1969): '[t]he Brighton
authorities proved a little sensitive to the picture I had drawn', as
Greene later remarked (*WE*, p. 78).

On the other hand, *Brighton Rock* is not a work of journalism
or social history any more than the subsequent film adaptations
are works of documentary. The Brighton in the novel is not merely
a popular south coast resort providing the backdrop for Greene's
tale: it is a state of being, a metaphorical evocation of morality and
amorality, of life and death. In this respect, Greene's Brighton is not
unlike Christopher Isherwood's Berlin in *Mr Norris Changes Trains*
(1935) and *Goodbye to Berlin* (1939). Indeed, its depiction at times
owes less to realism than to expressionism. As Cedric Watts explains,
'Expressionist art is characterized by the use of distortions which
evoke a deranged or unbalanced state of mind' (Watts, 1997, p. 176).
The recasting of Brighton as 'Greeneland' – with its broken landscape of 'flapping gutters' and 'glassless windows' (*BR*, p. 95) and
ironic place-names ('Paradise Piece', 'Peacehaven') – thus offers an
outward expression of the inner turmoil of the novel's main characters. As Greene later acknowledged in *Ways of Escape* (1980), 'the
setting of *Brighton Rock* may in part belong to an imaginary geo-
graphic region' (p. 77). Echoing the predicaments of its characters,
from Hale and the similarly ill-fated Spicer, to Pinkie and even Rose,
this is a claustrophobic place with a seemingly centripetal pull, where
'every road [...] ended on the front' (*BR*, p. 89). Of the main characters only Ida, who is from London not Brighton (even Hale, it is
suggested, has come from the 'same streets' as Pinkie [*BR*, p. 4]),
is free like the Whitsun day-trippers to come and go. The impression of ineluctable spaces and inescapable destinies is reinforced by
the depiction of neighbouring Peacehaven, the town to which Pinkie
and Rose 'escape' for a day trip: 'hundreds of feet below the pale
green sea washed into the scarred and shabby side of England' (*BR*,
p. 93). This is not a border to the sea, but a sealed-in place from
which there is for these characters no way out. Like the ever-present
sea in the novel, the influence of cinema upon the narrative is never
far away. Neil Sinyard has suggested that the expressionist aspects
of the novel can be traced back to an early encounter with German
Expressionism, in particular Arthur Robison's 1923 film *Warning
Shadows* (*Schatten – Eine nächtliche Halluzination*), which Greene saw

and reviewed in 1925. In his review Greene pondered how 'the gulf between naturalism and impressionism [...] can be brought in closer proximity'; he would later achieve this mixture himself in *Brighton Rock*, 'where a naturalistic landscape [is] charged with extremities of menace' (Sinyard, 2003, p. 44).

The novel was begun in 1937 as a detective story, with Ida Arnold as the sleuth (an unlikely mixture of Mae West and Miss Marple), Hale the victim and Pinkie the villain to be unmasked. Though Greene would later suggest that 'the first fifty pages of *Brighton Rock* are all that remain of the detective story' (*WE*, p. 60), some of its mysteries linger: for example, the circumstances of Kite's death and Hale's mooted involvement in it are anticipated and partly explained in *A Gun For Sale* but only alluded to in *Brighton Rock*. This is what Cedric Watts calls the 'transtextual' aspect of Greeneland: 'repeatedly [the reader] has a sensation of *déjà vu*' through Greene's use and re-use of 'certain locations, character-types and plot situations' (Watts, 1997, p. 152). Thus Rose can be seen as another of Greene's waif-like heroines, such as Coral Musker in *Stamboul Train*, Pinkie as another damaged, dangerous youth, such as Raven in *A Gun For Sale*, and Ida as another, more fully rounded iteration of the lascivious and charitable figure of Amy in Greene's 1936 short story 'Jubilee'. Like Ida the reader is implicated in a degree of detective work: why does Hale simply not flee Brighton in the first place, rather than stick to his 'Kolley Kibber' routine? And just what exactly happens to him? (It is hinted – but no more – that he has been choked with a stick of the town's famous confectionary.) In the 1947 film of the novel, some of these missing details are sketched in; for instance, Hale is seen disappearing into the ghost-train tunnel with Pinkie, who then pushes Hale to his death. Because the detective genre is a fundamentally conservative genre, being about the restoration of the *status quo*, the tying up of these narrative loose threads in the film can therefore be seen as playing to the generic origins of its source.

Brighton Rock also offers the first real exploration of the religious and theological terrains that would come to characterize Greene's fiction. Though Catholicism had figured in some of his earlier novels, in particular *Rumour at Nightfall* (1931) and *It's a Battlefield* (1934), in *Brighton Rock* the treatment is 'more radical and extensive' (Watts, 1997, p. 40). Not for nothing, then, does Greene date the moment at which he became labelled a 'Catholic writer' (*WE*, p. 74) to the appearance of the novel, and the association of his works with a particular brand of Catholic angst was later confirmed and consolidated with the appearance of *The Power and the Glory* (1940), *The Heart of the Matter* (1948), *The End of the Affair* (1951) and *A Burnt-Out Case* (1961). Throughout *Brighton Rock* there is a sense of theological and spiritual reflection. Pinkie is defined by his Roman Catholicism as much as by his experience of gang culture. However, Pinkie's religious beliefs are, to say the least, idiosyncratic. When Rose (also a Catholic) asks him if he believes in Hell, Pinkie replies:

> "Of course it's true", the Boy said. "What else could there be?" he went scornfully on. "Why", he said, "it's the only thing that fits. These atheists, they don't know nothing. Of course there's Hell. Flames and damnation", he said with his eyes on the dark shifting water and the lightning and the lamps going out above the black struts of the Palace Pier, "torments."
>
> "And Heaven too", Rose said with anxiety, while the rain fell interminably on.
>
> "Oh, maybe", the Boy said, "maybe." (*BR*, p. 55)

Pinkie, of course, means 'no'. This is reinforced later in the novel when he pointedly states: 'I don't take any stock in religion. Hell – it's just there' (p. 96). This is not a display of bravado: throughout the novel we see Pinkie drawing upon his Catholic upbringing and seeing the world in terms of its values – or rather his distorted, selective view of them. Pinkie's frightening vision presents a religion based on Hell: the hereafter will be an eternity of torment with no rewards or redemption. Believing that God has already decreed that he will be damned, Pinkie exudes a sense of predestination which is almost medieval and certainly pre-Enlightenment in its register, and later in the novel we get a fuller glimpse of this distorted theology. The corrupt lawyer Prewitt (another familiar inhabitant of Greeneland, the minor public schoolboy gone to the bad) is partly showing off his literary education when he quotes Christopher Marlowe's *Doctor Faustus* (c. 1604) to Pinkie, but it is a reference that has an acute impact on 'the Boy':

> "You know what Mephistopheles said to Faustus when he asked where Hell was? He said, 'Why, this is Hell, nor are we out of it.'" The Boy watched him with fascination and fear. (*BR*, p. 228)

Pinkie has earlier mistaken Prewitt's mention of *Hamlet*'s Polonius for the misogynistic slur 'polony' (*BR*, p. 227), yet he instinctively understands this reference. After all, he has lived his life believing that judgement has always been cast upon him and has gradually gathered a sense of what Hell really is:

> he had been afraid, afraid of pain and more afraid of damnation – of the sudden and unshriven death. Now it was as if he was damned already and there was nothing more to fear ever again. The ugly bell clattered, the long wire humming in the hall, and the bare globe burnt above the bed – the girl, the washstand, the sooty window, the blank shape of a chimney, a voice whispered, "I love you, Pinkie." This was hell then; it wasn't anything to worry about: it was just his own familiar room. (*BR*, p. 198)

For Pinkie, Hell is not fire and brimstone but the mundanity and the grime of daily, sordid existence – the dreary, downbeat features typical of Greeneland here chiming with his view of a fallen world.

Elsewhere, Pinkie is defined for us through another quotation, this time a corruption of Wordsworth's 'Immortality Ode' (1807): 'hell lay about him in his infancy. He was ready for more deaths' (*BR*, p. 70). (Greene mischievously substitutes 'hell' for Wordsworth's 'Heaven'.) Unlike the perpetually queasy old hand Spicer, Pinkie has an appetite for killing, though the narrative deliberately eschews the word 'murder' here – we have already been told that '[t]he word murder conveyed no more to him than the word "box", "collar", "giraffe"' (*BR*, p. 47). Almost comic in tone, this passage brilliantly announces Pinkie's complete lack of a moral compass. Yet Pinkie senses there will nevertheless be a chance of salvation, carrying in his head the (imperfectly remembered) words of the Elizabethan scholar William Camden like an incantation: 'Betwixt the stirrup and the ground/Mercy I ask'd, mercy I found.' As all of this suggests, Pinkie's reading of Christianity is not an orthodox one, but a composite, often contradictory (he conflates Hell with his earthly situation and yet fears for his salvation) interleaving of ideas dimly apprehended through half-remembered quotations from texts he has never properly read, and services in Latin 'speaking of things he didn't understand' (*BR*, p. 54).

The novel is the first of Greene's works to put forward the paradoxical view of the sinner who may yet be saved, a provocative theme that recurs in *The Power and the Glory*, *The Heart of the Matter* and *The End of the Affair*. One of the key metaphors developed in *Brighton Rock* is also an explanation of the title: when Rose reveals a belief that people can change (a more relaxed view of religious redemption than Pinkie's grim one of predestination), Ida counters her thus: 'Oh, no they don't. Look at me. I've never changed. It's like those sticks of rock: bite it all the way down, you'll still read Brighton. That's human nature' (*BR*, p. 216). Ida sees human beings as possessing a moral essence as inflexible and immutable as the letters that run through a stick of Brighton rock. Ironically, this is the one view of Ida's that the theologically and ethically inflexible Pinkie would probably share.

Though Pinkie might despise the irresoluteness of his fellow gang members, or resent the activities and attitude of his direct rival, the successful and monopolizing gang leader Colleoni, it is Ida who is his true nemesis, and this is underlined in their divergent attitudes to religion. Opposing Pinkie's unremitting commitment to belief, Ida instead favours a world of pseudo-spiritualism and ouija boards: 'She wasn't religious. She didn't believe in heaven or hell, only in ghosts, ouija boards, tables which rapped and little inept voices speaking plaintively of flowers' (*BR*, pp. 34–5); it is following one of these séances that Ida resolves to pursue Hale's murderer, and in due course, rescue Rose. As such, Ida's spiritualism is closely allied to her detective spirit, and in this regard her characterization echoes Sherlock Holmes's creator Arthur Conan Doyle, himself a keen amateur in the study of telepathy and the after-life. Her macabre interest in what lies beyond the grave, however, also serves to reinforce her commitment to earthly pursuits and pleasures: 'She liked a funeral – but it was with horror – as other people like a ghost story. Death shocked her, life was so important' (*BR*, p. 34). Ida, then, serves not just as Pinkie's nemesis but also as his polar opposite in almost every characteristic; like Pinkie, however, she is an ambiguously presented figure. Audaciously, Greene leaves it unclear as to with whom our sympathetic interests should lie.

Cedric Watts has suggested that in the characterization of Pinkie 'Greene seems to be conducting a taxing literary experiment: to see how far the reader's pity can be won for a person who seems to be irredeemably evil' (Watts, 1997, p. 172). Pinkie might not change and might be irredeemably evil, yet at the end of the novel there is the suggestion that he might also be saved when a priest comforts a grieving Rose: '"You cannot conceive, my child, nor can I or anyone the ... appalling ... strangeness of the mercy of God"' (*BR*, p. 268). The 'appalling' possibility that the murderous and unrepentant Pinkie could be admitted to Heaven is buttressed by our knowledge that the sense of peace these words bring will ultimately be denied to her, as the very last line of the novel affirms: 'She walked rapidly in the thin June sunlight towards the worst horror of all' (*BR*, p. 269): Rose is about to discover the true depth of Pinkie's malignity and hatred for her, inscribed on a cheap record as a memento of their wedding day.

In both film versions the ending of the novel is softened – notably, in the first instance, by Greene himself, who provided the screenplay for the Boulting brothers' 1947 adaptation (having rejected an earlier draft by the playwright Terence Rattigan). In this version the record is scratched, and the needle sticks: instead of the full impact of Pinkie's words, Rose hears an apparently benign message from beyond the grave, '"I love you" ... "I love you" ... "I love you."' The camera then pans up to a crucifix on the wall, suggesting that Rose has been saved from the 'worst horror of all' by divine means. Whereas the novel presents an ambiguous view, to say the least, of religious salvation (as Watts puts it, 'Who wants a Heaven that contains Pinkie?' [Watts, 1997, p. 97]), the film offers a less paradoxical, less troubling picture of Godly goings on. This film of a novel about Brighton razor gangs also found itself subjected to the slash of the censor, and the novel's portrayal of religion was again at issue here. As Quentin Falk notes, much of the novel's theological terrain was adulterated by the then British censor, Brooke Wilkinson, so as not to cause offence to the film's potential Catholic audiences (Falk, 2000, p. 46). Some other cuts to the film's theological content were administered by the film's director and producer, John and Roy Boulting, who felt that the novel's 'Roman Catholic mystical quality did not always ring true as expressed [...] by Rose and Pinkie' (Cited in Falk, 2000, p. 47). The overall effect is perhaps a little uneven. On the one hand, the film works to 'detheologize' the novel. On the other – and in stark contrast to what is suggested in the novel – it concludes with a possible miracle.

The ending aside, the film offers some other interesting deviations from the novel on which it is based. Whereas in the first chapter of the novel the focalization is entirely through the figure of Hale, the film does away with this, concentrating instead on scene-setting and exposition. As Quentin Falk remarks, 'After the first shot on the beach and a glimpse of a newspaper front page showing Hale's face and spelling out details of his stunt, we switch to the thieves' kitchen where Pinkie and his gang are deciding just what to do with Hale' (Falk, 2000, p. 46). This was Greene's own idea: 'In this way the boy is established before Hale who is after all a minor character' (R. Greene, 2007, pp. 136–7). In the novel, Pinkie's 'won't anybody stop that buer's mouth?' becomes – with a telling alteration – his first line in the film: 'Won't anyone shut that grass's mouth!' As well as altering the object of his enmity from Ida (in the book) to Hale (in the film), this also offers a knowing variation on the murder of Thomas Becket, 'Who will rid me of this turbulent priest?' – suggesting from the very beginning that the religious themes of the novel will also feature (albeit in attenuated form) in the film. This opening line also offers a partial explanation of what Hale has done to incur Pinkie's wrath – informed (or 'grassed') on the gang's activities in some way – something which the novel denies us. Similarly, whereas in the novel the death of Hale and its possible cause are only alluded to and never explained, the film again demystifies these for the viewer: 'In the film, [Hale] disappears into the ghost-train tunnel, with Pinkie slipping in alongside him in the open carriage. Just before the end of the nightmare ride, Hale plunges over the side and into the sea far below, clearly – for us – pushed by Pinkie' (Falk, 2000, p. 47). Pinkie then goes to a shooting gallery to seek an alibi from a disgusted barker, after which we see Pinkie being chastened by the other members of the gang for the murder. There is no equivocating over what has been done to Hale, or who has done it. Greene personally felt that the title lost some of its meaning with the relocation of Hale's murder from 'one of the small booths under the pier where Brighton Rock is sold' (R. Greene, 2007, p. 137). At the same time, however, as well as capturing the thriller dynamic of the story (Chibnall, 2006, pp. 63–4), the ghost train ride – appropriately called 'Dante's Inferno' – offers a visual correlative to the hellish imagery that abounds in the novel, and is an extremely apt location for the already-damned Pinkie to commit murder.

Pinkie's demise is likewise dealt with differently: the suicide 'pact' (Pinkie has no intention of killing himself) is moved from the cliffs near the ironically named Peacehaven to Brighton Pier, as Pinkie, cornered 'like some trapped animal, falls from the pier on to the steel girders and to the sea below' (Falk, 2000, p. 47). Although it might seem gratuitous, this shift of locale is germane to one of the key themes of the novel. Pinkie is as much part of Brighton as the sticks of confectionary (always *pink*, of course) that give the novel its title; he knows nothing but Brighton and its immediate environs, and in a revealing moment of self-consciousness he declares: '"I suppose I'm real Brighton", as if his single heart contained all the cheap amuse-ments, the Pullman cars, the unloving weekends in gaudy hotels, and the sadness after coition.' (*BR*, pp. 238–9). Pinkie is as fixed as the Palace Pier (a 'frustrated bridge' as the popular truism would have it), trapped and yet reaching out into nothing but the oblivious sea. The pier-as-bridge also offers another one of Greene's richly suggestive

border zones, 'the dangerous edge' between life and death, good and
evil, heaven and hell, and as such is an aptly liminal place for Pinkie –
whose eternal fate the novel leaves open to question – to meet his end.
In the Boulting brothers' film the acid (or 'vitriol') element is
eschewed altogether, and this is unsurprising given the graphic death
suffered by Pinkie in the novel:

> [Pinkie] said, "you bloody squealer", and put his hand up. Then she
> couldn't tell what happened: glass – somewhere – broke, he screamed and
> she saw his face – steam. He screamed and screamed, with his hands up to
> his eyes; he turned and ran; she saw a police baton at his feet and broken
> glass. He looked half his size, doubled up in appalling agony: it was as if
> the flames had literally got him and he shrank – shrank into a schoolboy
> flying in panic and pain, scrambling over a fence, running on.
>
> [H]e was at the edge, he was over: they couldn't even hear a splash. It
> was as if he'd been withdrawn suddenly by a hand out of any existence –
> past or present, whipped away into zero – nothing. (*BR*, p. 264)

This is Pinkie's death as seen from Rose's perspective. The passage
is particularly cinematic, presenting fragmentary glimpses of the
action, initially without interpretation (a 'police baton', 'broken glass',
Pinkie's screaming), leaving the reader to piece together what has happened: in the scuffle with Dallow and the chasing policeman, Pinkie's
bottle of vitriol has been smashed, and its contents have splashed onto
his face with devastating effect. The subsequent interpretation of
the scene before her – signalled by the twice-repeated simile 'as if' –
is clearly filtered through the prism of her religious belief, presenting an image of damnation redolent of the apocalyptic paintings of
Hieronymus Bosch (c. 1450–1516) or of Hans Baldung Grien's 'The
Ages of Man and Death' (1541–4). More than any work of noir or
crime fiction, furthermore, this ending resembles the finale of other
works of modern and mainstream gothic, from Matthew Lewis's
seminal novel *The Monk* (1796) to films such as *Ghost* (Jerry Zucker,
1990) or *Drag Me to Hell* (Sam Raimi, 2009), where another doomed
protagonist is similarly dragged by unearthly hands to an absolute,
fiery annihilation. In Rowan Joffe's 2010 film adaptation of *Brighton
Rock*, the full horror of this scene and its after-effects are graphically
captured, as the camera lingers on Pinkie's acid-mutilated corpse,
broken on the rocks under the cliffs at Beachy Head. Although it provides an unambiguous closure to his short and violent life, it is, like
the ending of the earlier film, not as powerful as the total *negation* of
Pinkie presented in the novel.

The Boulting brothers' film was not the first adaptation of *Brighton Rock*. This was a stage play by Frank Harvey which appeared in February 1943, while Greene was serving the British war effort in West Africa (an experience upon which he later drew in *The Heart of the Matter*). When Greene saw the production on his return, he judged it to be 'extraordinarily careless' (Sherry, 1994, p. 164) and even threatened legal action because of the perceived mangling of his novel: 'I am quite prepared to seek an injunction' (R. Greene, 2007, p. 125). He was particularly unhappy with the deletion of what he felt to be integral plot elements (notably the lack of an equivalent to the final scene in the novel, Rose's encounter with the priest), and with additions implemented by Harvey, at the behest of the play's producer Bill Linnit (including original lines given to the character of Ida). At one level, then, the Boulting brothers' film can be seen as having grown out from this earlier adaptation of the novel, taking members of its cast (such as Richard Attenborough's Pinkie and Hermione Baddeley's Ida) and 'correcting' its perceived faults (such as the restoration of the ending's religious slant). Greene's 'delight' with the ensuing film – 'the first time I have seen one of my own books on the screen with any real pleasure' (R. Greene, 2007, p. 147) – can therefore be set against his abhorrence of the earlier play version. This also echoes the relationship of the later Rowan Joffe version to the 1947 film: Joffe's *Brighton Rock* is an adaptation which has in mind a previous adaptation as much as the original text.

Joffe draws less on the novel than the 1947 film and Greene's screenplay for it, and this explains the similarity between the 'softer' endings of the two films: the final scene, featuring a clearly pregnant Rose and the equally pregnant recording given to her by Pinkie, but whose contents are mercifully (and it is implied, miraculously) never revealed to her, is the ending Greene wrote for the 1947 picture. Terence Rattigan, who wrote the first screenplay for the Boulting brothers' version, made Ida's accomplice Phil Corkery into a bookmaker, and Greene approved of this on the grounds that it tightened up the narrative (R. Greene, 2007, p. 137): Ida is, after all, an occasional gambler (her pursuit of 'Fred's' killers is partly in return for him having given her a good tip), and her relationship with Corkery gives her an insider's view of the racecourse world where Pinkie's gang operates. Similarly, some of the changes implemented in the 2010 film seem to have been made in the interests of tightening up the narrative (in particular some of its less convincing and more confusing aspects) and the relationships between the characters.

The beginning of the film still features the pursuit and murder of Hale. Yet this 'Fred Hale' is no longer the newspaperman of the novel but a rival gangland figure. The 'Kolley Kibber' plot device has been done away with, as has the mystery surrounding Hale's disappearance in the novel: in the film, he is unambiguously dispatched by Pinkie (Sam Riley) under Brighton Pier, bludgeoned to death with one of the beach's stones. Hale is killed by Pinkie for having killed Kite, the leader of Pinkie's gang, in the film's opening scene. This makes the motivation for Hale's death far less obscure than in the novel, closing up one of the 'gaps' in the original text where the reader is invited to furnish some of the meaning, while in addition fleshing out the character of Kite and the circumstances surrounding his death, both of which are deliberately given only the barest of outlines in the novel. In addition, Riley's Pinkie is not the blank-eyed, murderous teen of the novel. Clearly much older than Greene's Pinkie (Riley at 30 is almost twice his age), his killing of Hale is an apparently unpremeditated act. It is also a revealing rite of passage: through killing Hale he takes over leadership of the gang from Kite, whereas in the novel it is not altogether clear how Pinkie has gained his position of pre-eminence within the gang. In the novel and the first film Pinkie is compelled to marry Rose to prevent her testifying against him, after the gang's attempt to create a false alibi by depositing Hale's time-coded 'Kolley Kibber' tickets about the town goes awry. In the newer film, Pinkie's seduction of Rose instead centres on the attempt to retrieve an incriminating photograph – his accomplice Spicer (Phil Davis) has been snapped harassing Hale just prior to his murder by a seaside photographer. This is an adaptation of a later development in the novel, and is arguably a more plausible source of anxiety for Pinkie than the missing ticket of Greene's original – the photograph providing damning proof of the involvement of the gang in Hale's death.

Trying to deter his assailants, Hale cosies up to the timid waitress Rose (Andrea Riseborough) instead of Ida (Helen Mirren), who, in turn, is the manageress of the café where Rose works rather than the Whitsun day-tripper of the novel. This difference of occupation aside (Ida's occupation in the novel is, it is hinted, the oldest one), Ida's blowsy, investigative spirit, tenacious sense of justice and her network of useful male acquaintances are all retained: one of these is the bookmaker Corkery (John Hurt), whose characterization also borrows elements of 'Old Ghost', another of the men with whom Ida has romantic links in the novel. The focus of that investigative spirit, however, has been significantly altered: Ida is out to save Rose rather than bring the killers of Hale (whom, in another departure from the original, she clearly knows) to justice. Thus, whereas in the novel it is Hale's disappearance that impels Ida into action, in Joffe's film Hale simply disappears, an irrelevance to the plot.

A more obvious alteration concerns not the characters but the setting. Joffe has shifted the action forward some thirty years: the Brighton racecourse gangs of the interwar years have become the running seaside battles between Mods and Rockers of the 1960s. In this way the Whitsun crowds of the novel in which Hale tries to lose his pursuers have become in the film something that offers those same pursuers a screen for their own violence. In addition, whereas the novel's depiction of Colleoni is suggestive of the anti-Semitism of pre-war England, Joffe's characterization of Dallow (who is now of Afro-Caribbean origin) suggests the beginnings of a post-Windrush, more cosmopolitan era. Greene's novel is set during the depressed 1930s, and Joffe's 1960s setting likewise presents a picture of post-war decline, the Victorian slums which loom over Rose and Pinkie's upbringing ('Nelson Place' and 'Paradise Peace') having been replaced with the equally – if not more – squalid high-rise estate. Joffe's setting also recalls Pinkie's understanding of Prewitt's quotation from Marlowe, about hell and everyday life being one and the same. Pinkie's darkened, Hades-like basement-room lodgings are not unlike the underworld inhabited by Harry Lime in *The Third Man*, while Pinkie's belief in his own damnation is revealed and reinforced through telling visual details, such as the lingering image of the glowing electric heater as he and Rose commit the mortal sin of sexual congress outside of marriage. The timeline and the topography of Greeneland may have changed, but this remains the same, fallen world of the novel.

Exercises

- Both films of *Brighton Rock* drop the novel's early focalization of the story through Hale. Consider how this technical aspect of the story might be done on film. How would you present the by turns objective and yet subjective narrative perspective of the opening chapter of the novel on film?
- In the novel Pinkie and Ida are presented as being polar opposites of one another. How many of these oppositions can you identify? And how are these oppositions reproduced in either screen version?

- Consider the film versions of *Brighton Rock*. Does either present Pinkie in a sympathetic light? If so, how is this effect achieved? If not, how might this be achieved?
- Consider the influence of *Brighton Rock* on the landscape of post-war British fiction and film. Can you identify any other works of fiction or cinema that bear comparison (either in terms of characters, tropes or themes) with Greene's novel?

Chapter Four

The End of the Affair

The End of the Affair (1951) is the fourth of Greene's overtly 'Catholic' novels, a sequence that begins with *Brighton Rock* (1938), and also comprises *The Power and the Glory* (1940), *The Heart of the Matter* (1948) and *A Burnt-Out Case* (1961). Like *Brighton Rock* and, in particular, the film versions of that novel, it is concerned with issues of faith and belief and with the possibilities of divine intervention, and in the main protagonist's shift from atheism to the possibility of belief it anticipates *A Burnt-Out Case*. It is also the third of Greene's major novels about the Second World War after *The Ministry of Fear* (1943) and *The Heart of the Matter*, and in its representation of a love triangle during wartime it presages another, altogether more secular but no less angry work about war, *The Quiet American* (1955). The novel is arguably the most experimental among Greene's works in terms of style, technique and its approach to narrative form. It is the first of his novels, after the film treatment-cum-novella *The Third Man* (1950), to use a first-person narrator. It is also unique for being the most abundantly autobiographical his novels, and it has come to be regarded as a thinly veiled *roman à clef*. The novel was adapted soon after its publication by Edward Dmytryk in 1955, and for a second time by Neil Jordan in 1999, initiating a series of major adaptations of Greene's works during recent years which also includes *The Quiet American* (2002) and *Brighton Rock* (2010). As well as inviting comparison with the remarkable efflorescence of films of his works produced during earlier decades (perhaps most notably the late 1940s), this resurgence of interest in Greene has seen him re-packaged and presented for a new generation of audiences.

The End of the Affair is set in London during the Second World War. The narrator is Maurice Bendrix, a middle-aged writer who begins a passionate and tempestuous love affair with Sarah Miles, the beautiful wife of a civil servant acquaintance named Henry, in the summer of 1939, shortly before the beginning of the war. The affair runs for several years until it is ended by Sarah, abruptly, in June 1944, after Bendrix is almost killed by a bomb blast during one of the first V1 rocket (also known as the 'flying bomb' or 'doodlebug') raids on London: 'those strange new weapons that [...] droned steadily up from the south like bees' (*End of the Affair*, p. 54). After eighteen months without contact, and finding himself increasingly unable to move on from Sarah, Bendrix takes action. He employs Parkis, a private detective, to uncover Sarah's new love life. Parkis follows and spies on Sarah, and having gained the confidence of the Miles's maidservant purloins her diary. Upon reading the diary (which the narrative quotes from at length), Bendrix discovers what really lies behind the end of his affair with Sarah. On the night of the air raid, and believing Bendrix to be dead, Sarah promised God she would no longer see Bendrix if he survived the blast that should have killed him. Bendrix's 'rival' (to whom he gives the aptly cruciform name 'X') therefore turns out not to be another lover, but rather God. Moreover, Richard Smythe, who Bendrix thinks is 'the man for whom she had deserted me in June 1944' (*EA*, p. 60), is not another of Sarah's lovers but a religious sceptic to whom she had turned in a desperate – but ultimately futile – attempt to dissuade her of God's existence, thus rendering her promise to God null and void and allowing her to return to Bendrix. Bendrix's discovery comes too late, however, as Sarah dies suddenly of a chest infection. Bendrix develops a surprising friendship with the widowed Henry, and the two men grieve together. If Bendrix's survival of the V1 blast was a miracle, another is the disappearance, after having been kissed by the newly devout Sarah, of a hideous and disfiguring birthmark on Smythe's cheek ('His skin was quite fresh and young except for one insignificant spot' [*EA*, p. 154]). Another possible miracle involves Parkis's boy, who, suffering from suspected appendicitis, recovers overnight, claiming to have been visited in a dream and blessed by the spirit of the now-dead Sarah. The novel closes with the suggestion that the aggressively irreligious Bendrix may also have discovered, and then abandoned, religious belief, as he begs the God that has robbed him of so much to 'leave me alone forever' (*EA*, p. 160).

The 'affair' of the title, then, could be seen as referring not only to the end of an extra-marital romance, but also to the collapse of Bendrix's commitment to unbelief.

The novel was published the same year as the Festival of Britain, but its prevailing mood, like much of Greene's output, is far from celebratory. The violence of its wartime backdrop defines the context and mood of the narrative just as post-war chaos defines *The Third Man*, or interwar squalor defines *Brighton Rock*. The representation of London under siege mirrors the emotional crises of its main characters, from the division of Sarah's affections between her husband Henry, Bendrix and God, to Bendrix's uncontrollable hatred and jealousy at the infidelities which he imagines are being committed against him by Sarah. The destructive force that is the war and the destructive force that is their relationship are intertwined from the beginning. The war helps to bring Bendrix and Sarah closer together, the air-raids providing them with the opportunity for their trysts, just as it later helps to drive them apart, the promise made by Sarah to God never to see Bendrix again being necessitated by the bomb-blast that almost kills him.

Running parallel to the novel's vision of a romantic love suffused with and compromised by doubt and disbelief is its characteristically Greeneian take on the nature of religious faith. This is announced by the epigraph, which is taken from the French Catholic novelist, poet and essayist Léon Bloy, whose works promoted the spiritual value of poverty and suffering (R. Greene, 2007, p. 187): 'Man has places in his heart which do not yet exist, and into them enters suffering in order that they may have existence' (*EA*, p. xviii). For Michael G. Brennan, the 'latter half of the novel offers a rich miscellany of religious perspectives as it traces the painfully gradual process of Sarah (and, by implication, Bendrix) from doubt and despair towards the possibility of attaining Sanctifying Grace' (Brennan, 2010, p. 97). Brennan also finds Sarah to be, like *Brighton Rock*'s Ida Arnold, one of Greene's most interesting female characters:

> Sarah Miles, the most psychologically intriguing female character in Greene's fictions, has three devoted lovers. The first, in ascending order of influence, is her loyal but cuckolded husband Henry; the second is the infatuated Bendrix; and the third is God Himself who (at least in Bendrix's eyes) ultimately steals Sarah away from him. From the opening page of the novel, Bendrix envisages these three dominating presences in his life within a triangulated framework of doubt and hate. (Brennan, 2010, p. 93)

In addition to the three main protagonists, other characters such as the private detective Parkis and his young son who accompanies him in his investigations are important in defining the narrative and its exposition. Although Bendrix believes that Parkis makes an unscrupulous living rooting out adulterers, Parkis has a devotion to his deceased wife, revealed when he prays to her (and God and Sarah) when his child is seriously ill, and this has an important function in the novel. As Brennan points out: 'The purity of Parkis's love for his saintly wife counterpoints the self-destructive bitterness contaminating Bendrix's memories of Sarah' (Brennan, 2010, p. 96). Bendrix, of course, has good reason to be bitter. Sarah's illness is indirectly brought on by her seeking succour in religion – 'It was to his church that she had walked in the rain seeking a refuge and "catching her death" instead' (*EA*, p. 145) – and, in a further irony, it is exacerbated by her trying to avoid Bendrix as he attempts a reconciliation with her.

Various elements of Greene's other works come into play in *The End of the Affair*. The novel's complex engagement with the nature and limits of belief develops some of the themes explored in Greene's previous novel *The Heart of the Matter*, while Bendrix's agnosticism looks forward to the similarly sceptical Fowler in *The Quiet American* and Querry in *A Burnt-Out Case*. The emphasis on surveillance and subterfuge, including using 'code words' (*EA*, p. 41), 'plotting' with maids and 'powdering' doorbells (p. 48), is suggestive of the spycraft of *Our Man in Havana* (1958) and *The Human Factor* (1978) but put to use on a domestic level. The narrative's attention to the smashed topography of post-war London, meanwhile, as well as offering a projection of the broken lives of its main characters, carries with it strong echoes of earlier works such as *The Ministry of Fear*, also set during the Blitz, and later works such as 'The Destructors' (1954), set just after it. Greene had plenty of first-hand experience on which to draw here, having worked as a fire-warden off Gower Street in London during the war (Bendrix likewise has served 'in Civil Defence' [*EA*, p. 25]), and having seen his own studio in nearby Mecklenburg Square, where he had produced *The Confidential Agent* (1939) and *The Power and the Glory*, 'blown to pieces' during a raid (*Ways of Escape*, p. 88). This representation of a smashed London, the heart of Empire, can also be seen to reflect Britain's increasingly frail position as an imperial power, anticipating more overtly postcolonial works such as *The Quiet American* (set during the collapse of French rule in Indochina) and *A Burnt-Out Case* (set during the collapse of Belgian rule in the Congo). While London's Victorian architecture may seem resistant to the violence being wrought on the city ('the old Victorian stained glass above the door had stood firm' [*EA*, p. 54]), the Victorian certainties that once held up the imperial edifice – and which Bendrix notes in a photograph of Henry's father ('it was the Victorian look of confidence, of being at home in the world and knowing the way around' [p. 8]) – have long since been stretched past breaking-point. This erosion of old values and certainties is part and parcel of the novel's grapple with religion, clearing the way for the *deus absconditus* worlds of *The Quiet American* and *A Burnt-Out Case*.

The End of the Affair follows in the wake of modernism not just in some of its thematic preoccupations but also in terms of structure and style. One of the standout elements of the novel is the shift between the different narratives of the two protagonists. Although the shift is easily explained – Book Three of the narrative is Sarah's diary – it is nonetheless a radical, modernist moment, taking us from one confessional (Bendrix's) to another (Sarah's). It is an acutely self-conscious, at times metafictional work, the narrative occasionally pausing to pass comment on its own construction, and it often reads as a graph of Bendrix's emotions at the moment of writing ('I write the adjective with a sneer' [*EA*, p. 12]). Like Greene's next major work *The Quiet American*, the novel begins, as it were, at the end, working back to disclose through a series of flashbacks the series of events that have led to the crisis named in the title, and in this way the narrative is marked by that most modernist of technologies – cinema. In his 1980 autobiography *Ways of Escape*, Greene suggests that the structure of the novel remains for him one of its most pleasing elements: 'There is much I like in the book – it seems to me more simply and clearly written than its predecessors and ingeniously constructed to avoid the tedium of the time sequence' (*WE*, p. 136). As all of this suggests, *The End of the Affair* is one of Greene's most technically accomplished novels; Bendrix, tellingly, is also 'praised for his technical ability' (*EA*, p. 1).

According to Greene, the novel's cyclical, anachronic narrative structure grew out from his 'continual rereadings of that remarkable novel *The Good Soldier* by Ford Madox Ford' (*WE*, p. 136). The influence of Ford's celebrated 1915 novel can also be felt in *The End of the Affair* – and subsequently in *The Quiet American* – in the shift towards unreliable narrators and centrally pivotal and damaging *ménages à trois*. Of all Ford's works, however, *The End of the Affair* is perhaps most redolent of his 1909 collaboration with Conrad, the less well-known *The Nature of a Crime*. Both feature narratives written in the aftermath of, or the anticipated, end of an extra-marital affair, and a cuckolded husband with whom the narrator is friendly, and through whom he keeps tabs on his lover's whereabouts. Both feature narrators who question the existence of a divine creator, from the sceptical Bendrix in Greene's novel, to Ford and Conrad's self-styled (but similarly agnostic) gambler as 'Godhead', with his hands in the affairs – and the pockets – of others, and plots which pivot on dubious 'proofs' of that existence, from the appearance of a mouse in Ford and Conrad's novel, to an apparent miracle in Greene's. Moreover, both develop the theme that would become pivotal to Greene's works as a whole, the 'dangerous edge' which stimulates, and justifies, the narrator's existence: in *The Nature of a Crime*, the narrator has gambled with the fortune of his ward and risked catastrophic financial disgrace, necessitating the suicide with which his narrative – the confession named in the title – promises to culminate; in *The End of the Affair*, Bendrix and Sarah's trysts are carried out under the threat not only of being found out but of being rubbed out altogether by German bombs. At a significant level this *ménage à trois* on the page is mirrored by one off it. Ford, like Greene after him, was in thrall to Conrad, and Conrad's reputation as a modernist author owes much to Ford, who published Conrad in the *English Review* and the *transatlantic review*, which Ford founded and edited; Greene's entry into the interwar literary scene likewise owes much to Ford, who had helped smooth Greene's path to literary success after the successive failures of *The Name of Action* (1930) and *Rumour at Nightfall* (1931), when he gave a positive and influential review of Greene's 1934 novel *It's a Battlefield* (*WE*, p. 28). (Greene would later return the favour by re-introducing the then-forgotten Ford to late-twentieth-century readers as a director at the publishers the Bodley Head.)

 The End of the Affair also bears the imprint of Charles Dickens, with whom Greene had re-acquainted himself between finishing work on the film treatment for *The Third Man* and 'return[ing] to what I considered my proper job', writing novels (*WE*, p. 134). As Philip French points out, the figure of Parkis – recalling Perker in *The Pickwick Papers* (1837), Parkes in *Barnaby Rudge* (1841) and the Pawkinses and Pecksniffs of *Martin Chuzzlewit* (1844) – was 'so called out of homage to Dickens' (French, 2000). Moreover, *The End of the Affair* was the first of Greene's novels (and the second of his major works after *The Third Man*, written two years earlier) to employ a first-person narrator, a decision heavily influenced by his recent re-reading of Dickens's *Great Expectations* (*WE*, p. 134). This choice, however, proved an uncomfortable one for Greene: 'Many a time I […] contemplated beginning *The End of the Affair* all over again with Bendrix, my leading character, seen from outside in the third person' (*WE*, p. 135). Greene's struggles with this aspect of narrative form is particularly interesting given the discreet interplay between form and plot in *The End of the Affair*. Bendrix strives throughout to 'see' into aspects of Sarah's life which he is no longer part of or privy to – the removal of her diary, which is quoted at length by Bendrix and consti-tutes roughly a quarter of the novel's length, being a prime example; yet this, ironically, is precisely the kind of authorial power he imagi-nes his 'rival' God having. The limitation on perspective imposed by Greene's use of the first-person, that '"I" could only observe what "I" observed' (*WE*, p. 135), in this context seems particularly preg-nant, playing to Bendrix's sense of being able to know only so much about Sarah, and thereby to his sense of powerlessness and, ultimately, defeat.

The novelist and critic Francis Wyndham felt that *The End of the Affair* was hamstrung by the 'lack of detachment' created through Greene's use of the 'first person' (Wyndham, 1958, p. 22). The lack of an additional 'perspective' that Wyndham condemns, however, assists the novel in another dimension. Because both narratives are shot through with the emotions of their narrators, we cannot implic-itly trust either of them, and there is the suggestion – one encouraged by Bendrix's doubts – that the represented miracles are the products of the fevered imaginations (literally so, in the case of Sarah during her final days) of the narrators. Denied the authorizing, 'external' perspective of a third-person narrative, ambiguity is heaped upon ambiguity for the reader. Greene further muddied the waters of interpretation himself in the Collected Edition of the novel issued by William Heinemann and the Bodley Head, when he changed Smythe's 'strawberry mark' 'to a disease of the skin', 'which might have had a nervous origin and be susceptible to faith healing' (*WE*, p. 137) – raising the possibility of a biological explanation as well as a miraculous one.

As with many of his works, *The End of the Affair* also speaks to Greene's intertwined professional and personal lives. As Philip French explains, Greene had reviewed *Brief Ecstasy*, directed by Edmond Gréville in 1937, for the short-lived serial *Night and Day*, of which Greene was co-founder and joint editor: 'this melodrama concerned the adulterous affair between a handsome adventurer and the beautiful wife of a kindly, well-off older man who was incapable of satisfying her', and it 'anticipates the now much publicized postwar affair that Greene had with Catherine Walston, the young wife of a rich left-wing landowner, which provided Greene with the plot of *The End of the Affair*' (French, 2000). In a revealing acknowledgement of the novel's inspiration, and recalling the cryptonyms that Bendrix gives his imagined 'successors' ('X', 'Y'), *The End of the Affair* is dedicated 'To C'. William Cash's study *The Third Woman: The Secret Passion that Inspired The End of the Affair* treats this subject at length, and even goes as far as to suggest that adultery was for Greene a kind of literary catalyst: 'bad for marriage, but good for literature' (2000, p. 22).

In another link between character and creator, Bendrix's working methods precisely mirror Greene's own:

> Over twenty years I have probably averaged five hundred words a day for five days a week. I can produce a novel in a year, and that allows time for revision and the correction of the typescript. I have always been very methodical and when my quota of work is done, I break off even in the middle of a scene. Every now and then during the morning's work I count what I have done and mark off the hundreds on my manuscript. No printer need make a careful cast-off of my work, for there on the front page of my typescript is marked the figure—83,764. (*EA*, pp. 24–5)

The influential publisher Michael Korda later recalled watching Greene at work on *The End of the Affair* aboard the yacht *Elsewhere*, owned and operated by his uncle the film producer Alexander Korda, during the summer of 1951: 'the manuscript [ended], typically, with an exact word count (63,162) and the time he finished it (August 19th, 7:55 A.M., aboard *Elsewhere*)' (Korda, 1999, pp. 313–14). Bendrix's approach to the craft of fiction also carries with it much of Greene's strong belief, having been psychoanalyzed as a teen, in the power of the unconscious: 'So much of a novelist's writing [...] takes place in the unconscious: in those depths the last word is written before the first word appears on paper' (*EA*, p. 25). Hence, perhaps, Bendrix's fetish for blank paper: 'I have a passion for writing on clean single-lined foolscap: a smear, a tea-mark, on a page makes it unusable, and a fantastic notion took me that I must keep my paper locked up in case of an unsavoury visitor' (*EA*, p. 18).

The End of the Affair certainly has a strong claim to being the most autobiographical of Greene's novels. In October 1940, Greene's house at Clapham Common (the unnamed 'Common' in the novel) was, like Bendrix's Clapham residence, bombed. Catherine Walston, with whom Greene had recently embarked on a long and passionate affair, was like Sarah the wife of a politician, whose rise through the ranks is strongly echoed in his fictional counterpart Henry's passage from 'O.B.E.' to 'C.B.E.' to 'K.B.E.' (*EA*, p. 82). The novel has also been seen as an engagement with the ideas of the sceptical philosopher A. J. Ayer (R. Greene, 2007, p. 385), whose *Language, Truth and Logic* (1936) offered a dismantling of religious discourse, and who may have been a source for the 'tub-thumping rationalist' Smythe (*EA*, p. 140). In addition, Cyril Connolly, editor of the influential literary magazine *Horizon*, has been suggested as a source for Waterbury, who interviews Bendrix towards the end of the novel (R. Greene, 2007, p. 190).

Francis Wyndham felt *The End of the Affair* was an 'embarrassingly personal' novel (Wyndham, 1958, p. 22). Yet there are also as many departures from, as there are consonances with, 'real-life'. Greene did have an affair during the war, but with Dorothy Glover, not Walston, whom he did not meet until after the war, in 1946. Equally, when the novel appeared Greene was, as he later noted, 'happy in love' (*WE*, p. 140) – quite different from the broken and embittered Bendrix. Moreover, it was Greene's novels that had influenced Walston's decision to convert to Catholicism, which, though placing her closer to Sarah, seems to distance Greene even further from the unbelieving Bendrix. As the editor of the author's selected letters Richard Greene puts it, 'the difference between the novel and the lives that inspired it is considerable' (R. Greene, 2007, p. 138), and any attempt to read the novel through these lives is at best problematic.

The novel is as much an engagement with an established trope of modern fiction as with Greene's biography. Adultery is a theme rich for fiction, having the potential for plotlines of passion and betrayal, conflict and subterfuge. One of the most celebrated examples of 'adultery fiction' is Émile Zola's *Thérèse Raquin* (1868), a realist novel of sustained cruelty that remains shocking to the present day. Infidelity is the central theme of major achievements in fiction such as Gustave Flaubert's *Madame Bovary* (1856), D. H. Lawrence's *Lady Chatterley's Lover* (1928) and Ford Madox Ford's *The Good Soldier* (1915), whose influence can also be felt in the technical aspects of Greene's novel, as we have seen.

The influence of Greene's prodigious affection for and knowledge of contemporary cinema, as well as his reputed appetite for extra-marital flings, can also be felt on the novel. As Quentin Falk has pointed out, *The End of the Affair* could 'almost be a sequel to *Brief Encounter*' (Falk, 2000, p. 81), David Lean's 1945 film adapted from his own play by Noël Coward, with whom Greene would later collaborate on the film version of *Our Man in Havana*. *Brief Encounter* is about the non-beginning of what remains a chaste, unconsummated affair between Celia Johnson and Trevor Howard (who would later feature in the films of *The Third Man* and *The Heart of the Matter*); Greene's novel focuses very much on the consummation of, and ragged ends left by, the affair which might, in other circumstances, have taken place between Johnson and Howard.

The End of the Affair began to take shape in late 1948 during Greene's time in Anacapri, where he had bought a 'small house' (*WE*, p. 134), *Villa Rosaio*, with his proceeds from *The Third Man* (Sherry, 1994, p. 246). During this period Greene met the British novelist and exile Norman Douglas, and in 1949 was asked to write the screenplay for Douglas's novel of English expatriate life, *South Wind* (1917), for the Italian film company Lux Films (Holloway, 1976, p. 483). Greene therefore had films very much on his mind when he wrote *The End of the Affair*, which, unsurprisingly, is larded with references to cinema. Cinema offers Bendrix and Sarah an excuse for one of their first trysts: Henry 'didn't like the cinema and so she rarely went' (*EA*, p. 32). (In Neil Jordan's film, when Bendrix asks Henry, puzzled as to Sarah's whereabouts, if she is 'in the cinema', a certain duplicitousness on her part is implied.) Later, struggling to come to terms with Sarah's abandonment, Bendrix is confronted with evidence of her having apparently moved on in an issue of *Tatler*: 'Henry was successful now [...] here he was at the gala night of a British film called *The Last Siren*, pallid and pop-eyed in the flashlight with Sarah on his arm' (*EA*, p. 48). The title of this fictional film, while presumably referring to the alarm confirming the end of an air raid, also suggests how Bendrix, who feels 'incapable of lov[ing]' anyone ever again (p. 132), now perceives Sarah: she is the last of his lovers. Sarah's diary, purloined by Bendrix, records her visiting 'a news cinema in Piccadilly and s[eeing] ruins in Normandy and the arrival of an American politician' (p. 81); Greene hereby discreetly underlines one of the ways in which cinema had become integral to ordinary Britons' experience of the war. The influence of cinema can even be felt in Greene's dialogue, where Bendrix reassures Parkis that his son will not be exposed during the investigation to anything unseemly: '"This scene will have a Universal certificate"' (p. 60). This allusion to film classification is ironic, given the outrage attending the release of Jordan's much-heralded film version of *The End of the Affair* (1999) when the British Board of Film Classification, in a landmark decision, awarded the film an 18 instead of the anticipated 15 certificate. Greene was a keen advocate against censorship, as his intervention in the controversy surrounding the publication of Vladimir Nabokov's *Lolita* in 1955 shows [R. Greene, 2007, pp. 219–20]), and this decision no doubt would have had him joining the film's producers in protest.

Although not a sexually explicit novel, there is an explicit honesty in its sensuality:

> Henry had his tray, sitting up against two pillows in his green woollen dressing-gown, and in the room below, on the hardwood floor, with a single cushion for support and the door ajar, we made love. When the moment came, I had to put my hand gently over her mouth to deaden that strange sad angry cry of abandonment, for fear Henry should hear it overhead. (*EA*, p. 38)

The BBFC felt Jordan's film to be taking the sensuality of the novel a step further, and gave the film an 18 because of the perceived explicitness of its sex scenes. The BBFC's decision led to an intriguing debate about the adaptation – and about issues of censorship more broadly – played out in the national press between the film's producer Stephen Woolley and the former Benedictine monk and school head teacher Dom Anthony Sutch. Woolley was not merely surprised but 'appalled' by the BBFC decision:

> I expected an authorization of 15, as I was aware of two scenes illustrating the intimate physical passion that ignited the fictional affair between Bendrix and Sarah that are not suitable for young children. The final amount of nudity after the editing process was minimal. The film received a fitting 15 certificate in Ireland and an R rating in the US which allows anyone under the age of 17 to attend a screening if accompanied by an adult.

For Sutch the issue extended beyond the adaptation itself and into questions of reception. Sutch argued that film is in its essence more 'perilous' than the printed word:

> We must make a distinction between the written word and celluloid. The former enables the individual to create his or her own picture, while the film imposes a picture upon the person observing it. Film producers impose their own images into the minds of other people. In so doing, the film takes away the freedom of the young to make their own pictures. (*Guardian*, 2000a)

This is an age-old argument in defence of censorship which implies that literacy protects people in a way that beholding an image cannot. Edward Dmytryk's earlier film version of the novel also fell foul of the BBFC, for its religious rather than its sexual content. Falk notes how the British release cut the scene in which Bendrix condemns the priest, 'the British Board of Film Censors object[ing] to the spectacle of a minister of religion being subjected to dialectical attack' (Falk, 2000, p. 81). Yet the novel itself received significant ecclesiastical endorsement, winning the 1952 Award for Fiction from the Gallery of Living Catholic Authors (Sherry, 1994, p. 442), exemplifying the fascinating tensions and contradictions within Greene's life and works.

Censored or not, Greene had long maintained a strong disregard for film adaptations of his novels, and it is no accident that Bendrix shares this dislike: 'They were showing a film of one of my books at Warner's [...] The film was not a good film, and at moments it was acutely painful to see situations that had been so real to me twisted into the stock clichés of the screen. [...] I had said to her, "That's not what I wrote, you know"' (*EA*, p. 32). Jordan's film version borrows something of the novel's self-conscious, metafictional character here. When Bendrix takes Sarah to see a film based on one of his books, the movie they see is the Laurence Olivier-Vivien Leigh vehicle *Twenty-One Days* (1940). The film was directed by Basil Dean, with whom Greene collaborated on a dramatization of *The Heart of the Matter* during the writing of *The End of the Affair* (R. Greene, 2007, p. 166), and was scripted by Greene himself. Dissatisfied with his efforts, he took the unusual step of denouncing the film in a review for the *Spectator*. As he recalls in *Ways of Escape*: 'I had received a contract from [Alexander] Korda to write my second film script', 'and a terrible one it was, based on [John] Galsworthy's short story *The First and the Last* – Laurence Olivier and Vivien Leigh, who had much to forgive me, suffered together in the leading parts' (*WE*, p. 75). Perhaps stung by these recent difficulties adapting works by other novelists, Greene begged off adapting *The End of the Affair* for the director Edward Dmytryk.

Dmytryk's 1955 film opens with a panorama of familiar London landmarks (the 'stock clichés of the screen' mentioned in the novel) and a voiceover supplied by Bendrix, who, unlike Greene's narrator, is a former US serviceman: 'It began in London during the war. I had been wounded and discharged out of the Army, but I stayed on in London for I was a writer, and had become interested in another group fighting the battle for England's survival, the Civil Service.' A voiceover is also utilized when the narrative is focalized through Sarah and her diary, an analeptic shift heralded with a 'dream-like' fade. These concessions to the novel notwithstanding, the first-person frame narrative and temporal gymnastics have, for the most part, been done away with (although an early cut did include the use of flashback before this was dropped by the film's producers Columbia, 'much to Greene's disappointment' [Foden, 2000]). One reason for this lies in the perceived resistance of the novel to being adapted for the screen. Whereas earlier works such as *The Power and the Glory*, with its opening reminiscent of a tracking crane shot, were viewed as inherently 'cinematic' (and adapted accordingly), *The End of the Affair* – with its temporal contortions and 'unreliable' first-person narrator – was regarded as a more difficult work to adapt. As one contemporary reviewer put it: 'In general the works of Mr. Graham Greene lend themselves easily to adaptation for the screen; *The End of the Affair* [...] would seem an exception' (*Times*, 25 February, 1955, p. 11). This difficulty in reproducing the more technical aspects of the novel aside, the film elsewhere manages to capture the characteristically 'visual' quality of Greene's prose, as well as gesturing towards the inherent self-reflexiveness of the narrative. For instance, the leaves of Bendrix's manuscript – of a novel based on knowledge gleaned from his love affair with Sarah – are left scattered by the bomb blast, as if in comment on their destructive relationship. This act of textual destruction is reversed when the fragments of Sarah's letter to an 'admirer' – who turns out to be God – are rescued from the wastebasket and, like the ensuing narrative of Sarah's newfound relationship with God, 'pieced together'.

A more noticeable, and arguably less explicable, difference between Greene's novel and Dmytryk's film version lies the latter's choice of setting. Whereas in the novel the action takes place in and around Clapham Common in South London, in Dmytryk's film it is shifted to Chester Terrace, near Regent's Park in North London – or, as a reviewer for Greene's former employer the *Times* put it then, is 'unforgivably altered [...] to somewhere more fashionable' (*Times*, 25 February, 1955, p. 11). This alteration is perhaps not as gratuitous as it appears, however. A contemporary resident of Chester Terrace during the war was Sir John Salmond, former Air Chief Marshal of the Royal Air Force. Salmond had been pivotal in the establishment of the RAF as an independent branch of the armed forces after the First World War (when as the Royal Flying Corps it had been part of the Army), and had overseen the pioneering and controversial use of aircraft to suppress 'native' uprisings in British Iraq during the early 1920s. Whether intended by Dmytryk, the re-location (and bombing) of Bendrix's home thus carries with it a subtle comment on the origins, development, and use and misuse, of airpower on civilian populations.

There are much subtler alterations. Whereas in the novel Bendrix's limp derives from an unspecified childhood accident, in the film version its origins are more heroic: 'I got it early in the war.' (Bendrix's unbridled jealousy and paranoia with regard to Sarah perhaps suggest wounds suffered of a psychological kind, too.) In the novel Bendrix is a member of the Civil Defence, though his duties are not described; in the film version, he is explicitly made a fire-warden ('I'm getting a fine view of London roof-tops; if I were a painter I might be able to put it to some use'), a detail which seemingly draws as much on Greene's own wartime experience as on the novel itself. Whereas in the novel Bendrix is informed of Sarah's death over the telephone, in the film he is present when she dies. (He is, however, spared the sight of Sarah's ashes 'blowing over' [*EA*, p. 130] the crematorium gardens – a recycling of the newspaperman Hale's memorably evocative send-off in *Brighton Rock*.) On miraculously surviving the V1 blast, Bendrix recalls 'a terrific sense of space when I came to, like I'd been on a long journey', while his survival seems to resist medical explanation: 'They couldn't understand why every bone in my body wasn't broken.' Thus the film implicitly endorses Sarah's interpretation of Bendrix's survival as a divine intervention, eschewing the more sceptical approach of the novel.

Unfortunately for Dmytryk, the critics were, and remain, equally sceptical about his film. In spite of the strength of the cast – which includes respected and stalwart British actors such as Deborah Kerr (who turned down Hitchcock's *Dial M for Murder* to play Sarah), John Mills (Parkis) and Peter Cushing (Henry), and the US actor Van Johnson as the male lead – *The End of the Affair* was 'far from the toast of critics at the time' (Walsh, 1999). Greene himself took a characteristic dislike to Dmytryk's adaptation, as the novelist Giles Foden points out: 'In a 1984 Guardian Film Lecture, Greene described it as one of the "least satisfactory" of the adaptations of his religious novels' (Foden, 2000). After the prodigious success of the late 1940s, which saw several classic screen adaptations of Greene's works (*Brighton Rock* [John Boulting, 1947], *The Fallen Idol* [Carol Reed, 1948] and

The Third Man [Carol Reed, 1949]), the 1950s saw a series of under-whelming transitions from page to screen of Greene's fiction.

We can only speculate what Greene would have made of the second film version of *The End of the Affair*, released almost a decade after his death, in 1999. Adapted by Stephen Woolley and directed by Neil Jordan, it opened to almost unanimously positive notices, with both the film industry bible *Variety* and the *New York Times* calling it the best Greene film adaptation since *The Third Man* (Gillan, 2000). The opening of the novel can be read as a comment on the problems of adapting, as much as writing, an original work: 'A story has no begin-ning or end: arbitrarily one chooses that moment of experience from which to look back or from which to look ahead' (*EA*, p. 1). Jordan's film borrows this self-consciousness. Jordan called *The End of the Affair* 'Greene's best piece of writing' (Cited in Walsh, 1999), and his 1999 adaptation of the novel for the screen accordingly demon-strates an acute, and at times playful, knowledge of his source. At the end of Greene's novel, Bendrix begins to tear up and destroy his journal, which contains all his memories of Sarah, before relenting: 'for wouldn't that have been one more victory for Him, to destroy it and leave myself more completely without her?' (*EA*, p. 159). Unlike Sarah's diary, the contents of this journal are not repeated in the nar-rative, but only alluded to. Jordan's film, however, suggests that the narrative being unfurled *is* this journal. It opens with a close-up of Bendrix's desk, strewn with the accoutrements of writing – a pot of ink, a typewriter – and a piece of paper revealing the words: 'This is a diary of hate.' (The deliberate foregrounding of written text is also a familiar device in screen adaptations of literary works.)

Jordan's film follows a more evidently romantic structure than the novel, with Sarah dying of a protracted but unspecified illness near the very end of the film. The repeated soundtrack theme (by the British composer Michael Nyman) emphasizes that this is a pic-ture in the romantic genre like Lean's *Brief Encounter*, to which the film repeatedly alludes. This is tempered, however, by the decision to frame the narrative with Bendrix's overriding cynicism: the film opens with the words 'This is a diary of hate' and closes with the novel's final line, 'leave me alone forever.' Jordan's film is also inter-leaved with departures from the novel, some small and apparently insignificant (such as the alteration of the name of the Miles's maid-servant from 'Maude' to 'Suzanne'), others larger and more mean-ingful. As Jordan later put it in an interview given to promote the film's release in Britain: 'The main challenge was its status as a piece of literature – that is kind of intimidating. I've got a theory that if something is finished as a piece of perfect work there is no point in trying to do anything with it. In this case I felt there was something to be done' (*Guardian*, 2000b). Jordan's film also tackles the legacy and impact of the earlier film adaptation. The brilliant casting and performance of the American actress Julianne Moore as the cut-glass voiced Englishwoman Sarah, for example, can be taken as a playful reaction to the miscasting of the American actor Van Johnson as Bendrix in the earlier film. Ralph Fiennes, meanwhile, embodies the aloof cynicism of Bendrix in the novel just as Stephen Rea captures the harmless foolishness of Henry.

In Greene's original, Bendrix's works include *The Ambitious Host*, *The Crowned Image* and *The Grave on the Water-Front*. To this collection Jordan adds *The Vicarious Lover*, suggesting that, unlike the novel, Bendrix *did* get around to writing a *roman à clef* based on his affair with Sarah. Bendrix's limp, meanwhile, was acquired not through a childhood accident, but from having fought in 'Spain' – presumably the Spanish Civil War (1936–9) – situating him closer to real-life writers and contemporaries of Greene who saw service in Spain such as George Orwell and Ernest Hemingway, and further away from the politically disengaged and disinterested figures of 'Greeneland' such as Fowler in *The Quiet American* and Eduardo Plarr in *The Honorary Consul* (1973). As if playing on the hazy impreciseness with which Bendrix memorizes the address in the novel, Savage's detective agency is located not at 'either 159 or 169 Vigo Street' (*EA*, p. 17) but '3 Vigo Passage', as a close-up of Henry's well-thumbed business card reveals. The cinema to which Bendrix and Sarah go is not, as in the novel, the Warner cinema in Leicester Square, but the nearby Rialto, and they frequent the fictional eatery Palmer's, not Rules (which, in a case of life imitating art, now has a dining room named after Greene). It is Parkis's 'boy' Lance who now has the strawberry mark, not Smythe, who is no longer the 'crazy tub-thumbing rationalist' of the novel (in Bendrix's jealousy-distorted phrase), but a priest – the Father Crompton figure of the novel in all but name. Jordan apparently found Smythe's Damascene conversion in the novel problematic, and felt that if this was transferred to the 'boy' a biological explanation, rather than the religious intervention implied in the novel, would be more believable to modern audiences: 'I think those things do happen to adolescent kids, they go through changes in their lives' (Cited in Falk, 2000, p. 138). The transmigration of Smythe-the-rationalist into Smythe-the-priest is also a concession to the film's audience: 'The rationalist preacher character is quite confusing in contemporary terms, all that ranting in Hyde Park. It's one of those Greene creations that carries an idea but nothing more. So I merged him and the priest – now it's Father Smythe.' 'For the film I tried to keep the religious element very strongly in there, but more as an unseen protagonist than as a system of belief' (Cited in Falk, 2000, p. 138). This explains the reduction of the role of Father Smythe (played by Jason Isaacs), and buttresses the film's presentation of Catholicism as just another institution, like marriage, rather than a governing and inflexible framework. As Quentin Falk notes, Jordan had also briefly considered updating the material to a new historical setting, but could not think of a better alternative to the Blitz and, after this, the pilotless flying bombs which rain down on London (Falk, 2000, p. 138), thus enforcing the sceptical Bendrix's idea of a random universe, while offering Sarah the opportunity to revive her dormant religious belief.

There is one major difference between the novel and Jordan's film: Bendrix and Sarah recommence the affair. They leave London – to which the novel's setting is tightly, almost claustrophobically, confined – for a break in Brighton in order to plan their future together. There they visit the Pavilion, whose origins Bendrix (something of an expert on historical figures, as his biography of General Gordon reveals) enthusiastically relates to Sarah: 'Prince Regent began building it for his mistress Mrs. Fitzherbert', whom he had wanted to marry but, for religious reasons, could not. Instead, he 'married Princess Caroline of Brunswick, who was a Protestant [...] and built this huge folly to impossibility'. In the context of the renewal of their affair, this suggests a comment on how religion – in the shape of Sarah's promise to God – once threatened their own relationship. The threat, however, is not yet over. Bendrix soon discovers that Sarah is dying and that their plans for the future are for nothing: their being in this 'folly to impossibility', then, is also grimly ironic. The 'end of the affair' is not brought on by the inflexibility of Sarah's newfound commitment to God, as in the novel, but by Sarah's succumbing to illness at the point of their being reunited.

In the novel, much is pieced together after the death of Sarah: the meeting with her mother, the discovery of her childhood books and the scrawled patterns and sentences that flesh out the enigma of a lost love. Unlike the novel and the 1955 film version, Sarah's death, though unexpected, is by no means sudden, and Bendrix, having moved into the Miles's house at Henry's behest, is afforded time with Sarah as together they see out her final months. Significantly, then, Jordan's film follows other screen adaptations of Greene – notably *Brighton Rock* (1947), *The Heart of the Matter* (1953) and *The Quiet American* (1958) – in arguably softening the impact of the original ending. At the same time, this alteration is also in keeping with the deliberate reduction of the presence of Catholicism, and religion generally, by Jordan: 'towards the end of the novel there is a sense of Greene the novelist beginning to depart' and 'Greene the philosophic obsessive beginning to take over'; 'the series of coincidences that were revealed about Sarah's death and the [events] that led to her sainthood were slightly forced' (Cited in Falk, 2000, p. 138). As we have seen with the case of *Brighton Rock* in the preceding chapter, Jordan's interventions are also in keeping with the downplaying of the religious aspect of Greene's fiction in adaptations of his work on the whole. Some critics, however, disapproved of these interventions by Jordan. Stanley Kauffman, for example, felt the film 'trashed' the novel's subtleties and spiritual dimension: 'Jordan's screenplay is not an adaptation, it is a devastation. It's so drastic that we are left puzzled as to why Jordan, who also directed, wanted to adapt the novel at all if he was going to violate it this way' (Cited in Thomson, 2009, p. 207). Characteristically, the adaptation is unfavourably compared to the original work, the sanctity of which – using imagery borrowed from the work being reviewed – has been fatally compromised in the act of translation from page to screen. At the same time, it is nothing if not apt that these two films of *The End of the Affair* should cause a similarly schismatic reaction among the critics as did the novel itself. Whether in their 'original' or their adapted forms, Greene's works remain as stimulatingly provocative now as they did then.

Exercises

- Consider how the plot might be re-cast with a greater degree of objectivity (for instance, from the perspective of a third-person narrator). How would this change the story? What are the implications of actual or possible point-of-view with regard to the film versions?
- *The End of the Affair* is a novel with many 'secrets'. Drawing on the adaptations mentioned in this chapter – or other films you can think of – consider the strategies available for a filmmaker to articulate 'secrets' on screen.

- Bring together some of the characters and develop a scene that does not feature in the novel: for example, Henry discovering the affair and the subsequent encounter between him, Bendrix and Sarah.
- Consider Stephen Woolley's argument with regard to *The End of the Affair* that 'the sexuality in the novel and the movie, unlike most modern films, is placed absolutely within a moral and social context.' In what ways can this be said to be true?

Chapter Five

The Quiet American

The 1950s mark the mid-point of Greene's career as an author. The beginning of the decade saw the appearance of the penultimate of his quintet of 'Catholic' novels, *The End of the Affair* (1951), while its end saw him venturing up the River Congo in pursuit of the material that would later form the final part of this quintet, *A Burnt-Out Case* (1961). This was also a decade during which Greene continued to flourish as a writer of 'entertainments', most notably the darkly comedic works *Loser Takes All* (1955) and *Our Man in Havana* (1958). The decade also saw the publication of *The Quiet American* (1955). In its generic overlaps with the detective story and the thriller, its use of a war-torn colonial setting as a backdrop and a plot that pivots on a damaging *ménage à trois*, the novel bears comparison to preceding works such as *Brighton Rock* (1938), *The Heart of the Matter* (1948) and *The End of the Affair*. Yet *The Quiet American* also stands alone as the first, and arguably the most powerful, of his major political novels (a sequence that also includes *The Comedians* [1966] and *The Honorary Consul* [1973]). It is certainly the first of his major works to deal squarely with the subject of postcolonialism, being about the spread of anti-colonialism and the fall of empire, and the concurrent emergence of the United States as a global power in the years after the Second World War. It is one of only a handful of Greene's novels (along with *Brighton Rock* and *The End of the Affair*) to have been adapted twice for the screen, underlining its importance in the canon of Greene's works as well as its continued relevance through the years.

The Quiet American is set in early-1950s Vietnam during the last days of French colonial rule. It centres on Fowler (another of Greene's characteristically world-weary Englishmen), a correspondent for a British newspaper sent to cover the war between the ruling French and the communist Viet Minh. In spite – or perhaps because – of its dangers, Fowler has fallen in love with Vietnam, and intends to stay on in Saigon after the war: 'I wanted a day punctuated by those quick reports that might be car-exhausts or might be grenades [...] my home had shifted its ground eight thousand miles' (*Quiet American*, pp. 17–18). Having taken a Vietnamese lover, Phuong, Fowler writes to his wife in London asking for a divorce; his wife's Catholic beliefs, however, forbid this. Unable to promise Phuong marital commitment, she moves in with Pyle, a young American aid-worker new to the country. Pyle not only wants to win Fowler's lover, but Fowler's friendship, too. During an ill-advised visit to the north (near to where the French would soon lose the decisive battle of the war at Dien Bien Phu), Pyle saves Fowler's life when the outpost they are sheltering in is attacked. It turns out that Pyle is a keen student of the fictional American political theorist York Harding, who advocates a 'Third Force' made up of neither the French nor the Viet Minh, and sympathetic to American interests. Learning that Pyle is in fact a CIA agent involved in the installation of just such a 'Third Force', and that he is also behind a series of terrible bombings in Saigon, Fowler conspires with the communists to have his rival killed. The end of the novel sees Fowler, instead of celebrating news that he has been granted a divorce, and that his paper has granted him extended leave to remain in Vietnam, sadly contemplating his betrayal of Pyle. The story is related by Fowler who, utilizing a cinematic, flashback structure, begins as it were at the end, with Pyle already dead, before circling back to this point. As Philip French writes, 'this was only Greene's second novel to employ a first-person narrator and it unfolds like a movie in extended flashback with a world-weary film noir voiceover from Fowler' (French, 2002).

Greene's first novel to employ a first-person narrator was *The End of the Affair*. Yet whereas *The End of the Affair* is an often fraught engagement with the nature of religious faith and belief (the titular affair being ended by a pact with God), *The Quiet American* is 'the novel in which Greene decided to give God a rest', as Bernard Bergonzi underlines (2006, p. 148). Before starting work on the novel, Greene wrote to his lifelong friend and fellow convert Evelyn Waugh expressing his 'relief' at not 'writ[ing] about *God* for a change' (Cited in Falk, 2000, p. 137; emphasis in original). The rejection of God as a subject is perhaps echoed in Greene's choice of a first-person narrative

subjectivity, which eschews the God-like privilege of 'seeing' everything that is characteristic of his earlier works. Perhaps the most
notable example of this is the aerial – not to mention evocatively
cinematic – panorama which opens *The Power and the Glory* (1940),
providing what literally is a 'bird's-eye-view' of proceedings: 'A few
vultures looked down from the roof [...] One rose and flapped across the
town: over the tiny plaza, over the bust of an ex-president, ex-general,
ex-human being, over the two stalls which sold mineral water, towards
the river and the sea' (*Power and the Glory*, p. 1).

In his second autobiography *Ways of Escape* (1980), Greene
explains the source, and the desired effect, of his choice of the first-
person for *The Quiet American*. After finishing work on *The Third
Man*, 'I read *Great Expectations*. I had never before found Dickens a
very sympathetic writer, but now I was captivated by the apparent ease
with which he used the first person. [...] The first person had always
offered an obvious technical advantage': '"I" could only observe what
"I" observed' (*Ways of Escape*, pp. 134–5). This experimentation
with first-person narrative suggests a departure from the more objective third-person, 'camera eye' method with which Greene's fiction
was now firmly associated. Yet the cinematic is present in other ways,
as we will see.

In addition to Dickens, *The Quiet American* shares much with the
major political novels of Greene's mentor Joseph Conrad. Its central
theme of personal betrayal and political engagement are threads which
run throughout Conrad's *The Secret Agent* (1907) and *Under Western
Eyes* (1911). Fowler's ultimately futile policy of remaining politically
disengaged ('*dégagé*'), meanwhile, echoes the similar, and similarly
compromised, philosophy of the central character in Conrad's *Victory*
(1915). Greene certainly had Conrad on his mind during this period,
having been approached by his friend and collaborator Carol Reed to
help adapt Conrad's second novel *An Outcast of the Islands* in 1951
(Greene declined). Like *The Quiet American*, Conrad's novel is a tale
of cross-cultural love and betrayal with broader political ramifica-
tions, and is similarly heavy with Eastern exoticism. Yet if *The Quiet
American*'s internal politics of betrayal – of a philosophy, of a friend –
bear the imprint of the longstanding influence of Conrad, its wider
politics are very much of the real-world.

The Quiet American was Greene's second novel with a fully realized colonial setting after *The Heart of the Matter*. While *The Heart of
the Matter* is arguably more a 'Catholic' work than about colonialism
(George Orwell complained the novel might as well be unfurling in

suburban England as in Africa [Orwell, 1973, pp. 105–6]), *The Quiet American* is very much a meditation on imperialisms old and new. The novel draws upon Greene's first-hand experience of the collapse of French power in Southeast Asia. Greene first visited Vietnam in 1951 at the invitation of Trevor Wilson, the then-British Consul in Hanoi and 'an old friend of the war years' (*WE*, p. 154), while covering similar crises of colonial rule (the so-called 'Emergencies') in British Malaya and Kenya. He later served as a correspondent for *New Republic*, and in January 1954 visited the scene of what two months later would prove the decisive battle of the French war, Dien Bien Phu. After the French withdrawal, Greene 'took tea' with the new President of Vietnam, Ho Chi Minh, underlining his apparent lack, like Fowler, of political iden-tification with either side (*WE*, p. 157). Greene also wrote pieces on the war for *Paris Match*, the *Listener* and – notably – the *Times*. As the first newspaper to send its correspondents to war (when W. H. Russell covered the Crimean War [1853–6]), the *Times* began the tradition of war reportage which has seen Fowler despatched to Vietnam. Fowler's description of his London office, moreover ('that grim Victorian building near Blackfriars station with a plaque of Lord Salisbury by the lift' [*QA*, p. 58]), suggests his employer is in fact the *Times*. In the dedication Greene stresses that 'this is a story and not a piece of history' (*QA*, p. xv). Yet many of the episodes in the novel – perhaps most notably the 'bicycle bombs' and the larger bomb-blast 'near the Continental' which pushes Fowler into taking sides – were based not only on real events, but also on events witnessed by Greene. The aerial bombing of a village 'near the Chinese border' (p. 140) by the French, for example, is an almost verbatim repetition of Greene's 'A Memory of Indo-China', an article published in the 15 September 1955 issue of the *Listener*.

The novelist Francis Wyndham argued that *The Quiet American* was let down by the eponymous character: Pyle is 'flatly conceived' and a 'caricature' (Wyndham, 1958, p. 24). The characterization of Pyle proved hugely problematic not only for critics of the novel but also for those working on subsequent screen adaptations of it. As Christopher Hampton, who adapted the 2002 version directed by Phillip Noyce, puts it: '"It's the American who gives you the trouble"' (Cited in Sinyard, 2003, p. 160). Yet Pyle's 'flatness' and proximity to caricature, to use Wyndham's terms, are perhaps precisely the point. As Edward Said has suggested elsewhere, Greene seems to have intended that Pyle should be seen as a cypher. For if Fowler's ageing imperialist embodies Britain's post-imperial decline, Pyle exemplifies the overweening 'exceptionalism' (Said, 1994, p. 290) that Greene felt was one of the most dangerous aspects of American power: as the quiet American of the title, Pyle embodies an imperialism that dare not speak its name but masquerades as something else. Indeed, from the opening scene where Fowler watches the unloading of 'the new American planes' – aid to the ailing French war effort – down by 'the river-front' (*QA*, p. 3), the novel is attentive to America's increasing military and political presence in Southeast Asia – a presence that would escalate during the coming years with the Vietnam War (c. 1965–75). Like *Our Man in Havana*, whose depiction of Western unease over secret weapons on the island of Cuba can be seen to anticipate the Cuban Missile Crisis of 1962, *The Quiet American* is a work of considerable political astuteness and foresight, and it was not long before contemporary commentators began to take note. As Michael Herr put it in *Dispatches* (1978), his classic piece of Vietnam War reportage:

> You couldn't find two people who agreed about when [the war] began [...] Maybe it was already over for us in Indochina when Alden Pyle's body washed up under the bridge at Dakao, his lungs full of mud; maybe it caved in with Dien Bien Phu. But the first happened in a novel, and while the second happened on the ground it happened to the French, and Washington gave it no more substance than if Graham Greene had made it up too. (Herr, 1978, p. 46)

Herr underlines here the close interplay of literary fiction and political history in Greene's novel. Some critics, however, equated the political vision put forward in it with the personal views of its author.

Many critics came to view *The Quiet American* as an anti-Americanist work. This perceived anti-Americanism certainly coloured early notices of the novel in the United States, most notably A. J. Liebling's scathing 1956 review in *The New Yorker*, entitled 'A Talkative Something-or-Other'. (Liebling later altered the title of his review to 'A Talkative Jerk' for a 1963 collection of his journalism, providing a measure of his own antipathy towards Greene.) This negative reception in America also had a clear political element, with some critics viewing the novel – by an author who made no secret of having briefly been a member of the Communist Party while at Oxford, an affiliation which saw him deported from the US territory of Puerto Rico under the McCarran Act just prior to its publication (*WE*, p. 210) – as a *pro-communist* work. This reaction is enshrined in the title of a notice which appeared in a contemporary edition of *Newsweek*: 'When Greene is

Red' (Cited in Sherry, 1994, p. 473). Pointing to an early film review in which Greene had condescendingly referred to 'the eternal adolescence of the American mind', Greene's biographer Norman Sherry even goes so far as to suggest that this supposed anti-Americanism on Greene's part has a cinematic explanation: 'Greene's strong and bitter dislike of certain aspects of American life and culture [...] must have stemmed from seeing countless American movies' (Sherry, 1989, p. 593). This argument seems counterintuitive: it follows that if Greene loved the cinema, one of America's main cultural products and exports, he could not have wholly disliked America. Nevertheless, Sherry's point underlines the perceived anti-Americanism that has coloured discussion of the novel.

Despite having had fairly mixed reviews after its publication in Britain in December 1955 and in America in March the following year (Sherry, 1994, p. 472), *The Quiet American* has since 'been elevated to the status of one of Greene's major works' (Pratt, 1996, p. xiii). As the novelist Zadie Smith put it recently, 'one can imagine nobody who could better weave the complicated threads of war-torn Indochina into a novel as [...] thematically compact and as *enjoyable* as *The Quiet American*' (Smith, 2004, p. xi; emphasis in original). As with *The Third Man*, the title of the novel has since entered the language. In a particularly notable example, at the peak of the Vietnam War, Greene's old employer the *Times* labelled Spiro Agnew, Richard Nixon's bullish Vice President, 'the unquiet American' (10 January 1970, p. 9).

Basil Wright has argued that Greene always 'had a built-in filmic style', a style drawing, no doubt, on Greene's early experiences as a film critic – and, it must be added, on his deliberately conceiving early works such as *Stamboul Train* with their eventual adaptation for the screen in mind. Wright argues that this 'cinematic approach' is 'fined down to the exquisite "chinese box" flashback technique in [...] *The Quiet American*' (Cited in Falk, 2000, p. 4). Greene draws on his knowledge and experience of cinema for *The Quiet American*'s narrative structure, as well as some of the novel's many memorable images. For example, the antique press used to create the bicycle bombs is described by Fowler as having belonged 'to the same era as the nickelodeon' (*QA*, p. 136). Meanwhile, revealing something of Fowler's own cinematic tastes (and prejudices), the Caodist festival at the Holy See in Tanyin is compared to 'a Walt Disney fantasia of the East, dragons and snakes in technicolour' (p. 75). And, in a particularly striking and evocative image, during the attack on the watch-tower on the road back from Tanyin, Fowler, his ankle broken, recalls flitting in and out of consciousness thus: 'Then he [Pyle] simply went out like a picture on the screen when the lamps of the projector fail: only the soundtrack continued' (p. 99). In fact the cinema is in many ways part of the novel's narrative texture. Pyle appears to Fowler to be taking his heroic cue during the watch-tower attack from having seen too many 'war-films' ('We aren't a couple of marines and you can't win a war-medal' [p. 102]). Phuong is also a keen cinephile: the end of the novel has her returning from having seen a film of the French Revolution ('"the people [...] were singing the Marseillaise"' [p. 178]) – another violent, epochal moment, like the implosion of French rule in Southeast Asia depicted in the novel, in the modern history of France.

The novel's orientalizing presentation of Vietnam is also strikingly cinematic. Fowler refers to 'the real background' of Vietnam 'that held you as a smell does':

> the gold of the rice-fields under a flat late sun: the fishers' fragile cranes hovering over the fields like mosquitoes: the cups of tea on an old abbot's platform, with his bed and his commercial calendars, his buckets and broken cups and the junk of a lifetime washed up around his chair: the mollusc hats of the girls repairing the road where a mine had burst: the gold and the young green and the bright dresses of the south, and in the north the deep browns and the black clothes and the circle of enemy mountains and the drone of planes. (*QA*, p. 17)

Fowler reduces Vietnam to an impressionist, exoticized image of the East. Likewise, there is a general sense of the comparative anonymity of the Vietnamese, who may form the 'real background' but are *only* background. This flatness of characterization seemingly creeps into Fowler's description of his communist contact Mr Chou: 'He seemed to take up no room at all: he was like the piece of grease-proof paper that divides the biscuits in a tin. The only thickness he had was in his striped flannel pyjamas' (*QA*, p. 117). Like other women in Greene (with the exception of *Brighton Rock*'s Ida Arnold and *The End of the Affair*'s Sarah Miles), Phuong is an enigmatic, even shadowy figure, as her first appearance in the novel seems to register: 'I saw a girl waiting in the next doorway. I couldn't see her face, only the white silk trousers and the long flowered robe, but I knew her for all that' (*QA*, p. 3).

According to Peter Mudford, Phuong is 'a character whom Greene sees as an "object" rather than a person in the new world order' (Mudford, 1996, p. 42). For Mudford, however, what 'might seem a weakness in Greene's ability to create Phuong from within in fact portrays the shift from a romantic view of marriage to a practical and commercial contract of which the purpose is migration' (p. 43). Or to put it more plainly: 'the young woman wants nothing so much as to get [. . .] out of Vietnam, which the French are losing to the Communist insurgents from the north' (Queenan, 2002). Phuong's obsession with the products of Western culture such as the illustrated press and photographic 'picture books' (which the 1958 film retains) and, in particular, the cinema of Hollywood and Europe, can therefore be seen to be nourishing an image of 'the West' which Phuong sees as her eventual destination, whether married to Pyle or to Fowler. Phuong's continual confusion of American and European landmarks, which Fowler condescendingly puts down to her being 'wonderfully ignorant' of geography (*QA*, p. 4), might best be understood in this context of marriage, migration, and escape: for her they are one and the same, an idea of the West qualitatively different, and infinitely preferable, to her present Eastern reality. Phuong's name, which translates as 'phoenix' (p. 3), suggesting reinvention and renewal, is therefore a particularly apt one.

Fowler uses the titular phrase of the novel to distinguish Pyle from his stereotypically noisy compatriots ('"Not one of those noisy bastards at the Continental. A quiet American"' [*QA*, p. 9]), and Vigot uses it euphemistically to refer to the now-dead Pyle ('"Yes. [...] A very quiet American"' [p. 9]). Yet, as Fowler reveals, it is in fact Phuong who supplies Pyle with his moniker and the novel with its title: '"He's quiet", she said, and the adjective which she was the first to use stuck like a schoolboy name' (p. 29). In many ways Phuong is herself silent in that she is deprived of a voice. The reasons, and cultural meanings, of this lack are varied. There is, of course, a general issue surrounding problems of language and communication: neither Pyle nor Fowler speak Vietnamese, and only Fowler can speak colonial French with her; Fowler recollects 'that first tormenting year when I had tried so passionately to understand her, when I had begged her to tell me what she thought and had scared her with my unreasoning anger at her silences' (*QA*, pp. 124–5). These language barriers give rise to a wryly comic scene where Fowler translates Pyle's romantic overtures to Phuong on behalf of his rival. On the one hand, Greene's novel (like the subsequent film adaptations which further reduce Phuong's role) could be seen to be reproducing the familiar Orientalist trope of the 'inscrutable' Eastern other. On the other, a postcolonial sensibility with regard to the politics of representation could also be at issue, whereby the novel does not presume fully to know or to 'speak' for that other. Putting these cross-cultural issues aside, there is, at bottom, a more broadly humanistic element to Fowler's grapple with representing Phuong. As he ruefully acknowledges: 'I knew I was inventing a character just as much as Pyle was. One never knows another human being' (*QA*, p. 124). One of the main criticisms of both the 1958 and 2002 adaptations of Greene's novel for the screen, that in each Phuong is more a cypher than a fully realized character, thus indirectly speaks to these problems of representation explored in the novel.

The 1958 film adaptation of Greene's novel was also marked by a clash of viewpoints. It was adapted and directed by Joseph Mankiewicz, whose recent directing credits had included *The Barefoot Contessa* (1954), *Guys and Dolls* (1955) and the Oscar-winning *All About Eve* (1950), and whose final directing credit, *Sleuth* (1972), starred Michael Caine, who would go on to play Fowler in the 2002 film version of *The Quiet American*. The evocative monochrome cinematography was provided by Robert Krasker, who had also shot Carol Reed's *Odd Man Out* (1947) and – notably – *The Third Man* (1949). Krasker's 'images give Mankiewicz's film the sharp, high-contrast look of black and white newsreel' (French, 2002), which speaks to Fowler's (and Greene's) profession as a journalist and, by extension, his supposedly personally disinterested and politically detached viewpoint ('I wrote what I saw. I took no action—even an opinion is a kind of action' [*QA*, p. 20]). In a 1935 film review, Greene had pointedly asked whether the new colour cinematography could reproduce 'the suit that has been worn too long, [or] the oily hat' (*Pleasure-Dome*, p. 10), a comment that recalls the cheap suits and frayed cuffs of *England Made Me*'s Anthony Farrant, *Brighton Rock*'s Pinkie, *The Third Man*'s Rollo Martins and the similarly shabby Fowler in *The Quiet American*. More generally, then, Krasker's monochrome palette suited Greene's fiction because, unlike Technicolor (or 'technihorror' as Greene called it [*Pleasure-Dome*, p. 10]), it more closely conveyed the characteristic seediness of 'Greeneland'.

Yet despite this pedigree, Greene loathed the resulting film, later referring to the 'treachery' (*WE*, p. 15) of Mankiewicz's adaptation (an apt phrase given the themes of loyalty and betrayal explored in the adapted text). Greene's taking a dislike to an adaptation of one of his works was hardly new. Indeed, his opinion that the screen version of *The Third Man* was an improvement on the book ('Preface', *The Third Man and The Fallen Idol*, p. 4), like his approval of the Boulting brothers' version of *Brighton Rock* (1947), suggestively stand alone.

He described the adaptation of his first novel *The Man Within* (1929) by Sidney Box as a piece of 'treachery to my first-born' (*WE*, p. 15), and ever since *Stamboul Train* (1932), the first of his works adapted for the cinema, had come to feel that his novels had been generally ill served by their big screen incarnations. Yet as Greene suggests in *Ways of Escape*, Mankiewicz's film would always serve as the yardstick by which he measured other 'bad' adaptations of his work (p. 15). In his 1958 essay 'The Novelist and the Cinema', Greene reflects on the cruel and capricious nature of adaptation: 'a writer should not be employed by anyone but himself. If you are using words in one craft, it is impossible not to corrupt them in another medium under direction. [...] This is the side of my association with films that I most regret' (Cited in Falk, 2000, p. 5). Tellingly, Greene's essay appeared the same year as Mankiewicz's film of *The Quiet American*: Greene clearly had Mankiewicz in his sights here. The fact that Greene reiterates this negative view in *Ways of Escape*, published some twenty years after this essay, suggests that any resentment at the 'treachery' done to the novel, instead of fading over time, had merely percolated. Mankiewicz, for his part, later called it '"a very bad film I made during a very unhappy time in my life"' (Cited in French, 2008).

The film was shot partly in Rome and on location in Saigon. Much like the battle-scarred post-war Vienna of *The Third Man*, Saigon had changed little since the collapse of French rule a mere four years before shooting began, providing an 'authentic' backdrop for filming Greene's novel. There were, however, some slight problems to negotiate, as Michael Redgrave, who played Fowler, later recalled. Although 'Vietnam, following the Geneva peace conference three years before', was now 'a divided country', '[t]here seemed little trace of the war that had been fought or the war that was to come':

> Only once did we see a sign of the conflict. It was whilst we were shooting the [opening] scenes of the Indo-Chinese New Year. Placards borne aloft in a religious demonstration were suddenly turned around, revealing on their reverse side anti-Government slogans. When this was pointed out and interpreted for us, someone shouted we should have to cut those shots, or else re-shoot them. "Leave them in", said [Mankiewicz]. [...] "What the hell? No one'll know what they mean." (Redgrave, 1983, pp. 215–16)

In a letter to the *Times* from 1957, Redgrave wrote that 'films of well-known novels always arouse a host of people who are prepared to wager that "they won't get it right."' The production of *The Quiet American*, however, was, he felt, marked by 'a desire to get things right' that extended beyond merely capturing 'local colour' (*Times*, 29 January 1957, p. 9).

Indeed, Mankiewicz's film follows the novel with considerable attention, but with one key – and for Greene particularly galling – exception. There are, inevitably, some small concessions: there is no indication that Redgrave's Fowler is an opium addict, and Claude Dauphin's Vigot, the French Sûreté (colonial police) chief who suspects Fowler's involvement in Pyle's murder, no longer conspicuously reads the philosophy of Pascal (though another officer expresses a preference for the poetry of Alphonse de Lamartine: 'it is an escape, like whisky'). The novel's ending, however, had in Greene's words been 'turned upside down' (Cited in Falk, 2000, p. 137). Instead of the shadowy CIA operative of the novel, Pyle is revealed to be a guiltless victim, framed by the communists. In the novel, Pyle supplies his 'Third Force' representative General Thé with plastic explosives, which Thé indiscriminately uses to bomb civilians, blaming these atrocities on the communists; in the film, Pyle (working this time for the more philanthropic-sounding 'Friends for Free Asia' rather than the 'Economic Mission' of the novel) is an importer of plastics, but with the innocent aim of making children's toys for the Chinese New Year celebrations – the same celebrations with which Mankiewicz's film opens. In the novel, Fowler betrays Pyle by reading a passage from 'Dipsychus' (1850) by the Victorian poet A. H. Clough; in the film, Fowler reads a passage about jealousy from Shakespeare's *Othello*, indicating he is betraying Pyle more for personal than political reasons. To compound Fowler's error and misery, Phuong returns to her former life as a dance hostess following Pyle's death, never to speak to him again. In the novel, Fowler successfully recaptures Phuong's affections, but at the expense of some essential part of himself; in the film, he is left physically as well as emotionally isolated, shunned by his lover and companion, and having had his friend and rival killed on an erroneous premise. As such, Fowler's last words in the novel, which are also the last words in Mankiewicz's screenplay – 'I wished there existed someone to whom I could say that I was sorry' (*QA*, p. 180) – retain their charge, though their significance is ironically changed. Conversely, this example also underlines where Mankiewicz's screenplay, which borrows much of Greene's original dialogue, stays true to the novel.

Fritz Lang's 1944 adaptation of Greene's *The Ministry of Fear* (1943), a thriller set during the London Blitz, altered the novel's ending because 'no studio would then countenance a finale as bleak and compromised as Greene's' (Patterson, 2002). Mankiewicz's *The*

Quiet American, on the other hand, bent less to studio pressures
than to the wider political climate of mid-1950s America, which was
deeply anti-communist following the rise of the Republican Senator
Joseph McCarthy and the House Un-American Activities Committee
hearings – not to mention the recently ended Korean War (1950–3),
the first 'hot' conflict of the Cold War ('in those days [...] all the
world wanted to read about was Korea' [*QA*, p. 36]). As Quentin
Falk glosses, in the translation from page to screen 'the story was
switched from being anti-American [...] to being specifically anti-
communist' (Falk, 2000, p. 97), moving the film closer to the explicit
propaganda of Alberto Cavalcanti's *Went the Day Well?* (1942), an
adaptation of Greene's short tale about German fifth columnists in
wartime England, and away from the political percipience of the original. Nevertheless, *The New Yorker*'s influential film critic Pauline
Kael argued that despite this fundamental change Mankiewicz's film
remains, like the novel, about the harm that 'crusading idealism' can
do (Kael, 1965, p. 336): here, however, the crusader is Fowler.

The casting of Audie Murphy, America's most decorated hero of
the Second World War, as Pyle also proved to be provocative, not
least with Michael Redgrave, who in his autobiography later complained of his co-star's 'woodenness' as an actor: 'I'll never adjust to
the problem of acting with someone like Murphy, a "natural" with
a mass of experience but no technique' (Redgrave, 1983, p. 216).
Others have found Murphy to be 'an evocative piece of casting': 'a
true American hero playing a blandly evil man (at least until the cli-
mactic [narrative] acrobatics), with a *tabula rasa* face upon which anything can be read' (Patterson, 2002). Jonathan Nashel has suggested
that Greene's description of Pyle's 'unused face' (*QA*, p. 9) may
derive from the description of the Devil in Herman Melville's *The
Confidence-Man: His Masquerade* (1857): 'His cheek was fair, his chin
downy, his hair flaxen' (Nashel, 1996, p. 325). This is, of course, also
a common trope in Greene: the featureless 'innocent' face on which
experience has yet to draw its contours, from Pinkie in *Brighton Rock*
to Wilson in *The Heart of the Matter*. If Redgrave as the cynical and
disillusioned Fowler is 'one of a handful of [quintessential] cinematic
Greenelanders' (Patterson, 2002), it could be argued that so, too, is
Murphy. Rather than lessening the impact of the film of the novel,
Murphy's blank 'unreadability' in fact brings the film closer to it.

In the novel, Fowler's oafish fellow reporter Granger – who unlike
Pyle is very much an *unquiet* American – makes a passing but telling reference to Stephen Crane's American Civil War novel *The*

Red Badge of Courage (1895), and with it, to a literary tradition of representing war (*QA*, p. 28). As well as belonging itself to this tradition, Greene's novel can also be seen as having had a shaping effect on some of the later attempts at representing war which followed, in particular of the American war in Vietnam. In *Dispatches*, Michael Herr notes that every journalist covering the Vietnam War seemed to carry a copy of *The Quiet American* in his knapsack (p. 46); Herr, of course, later scripted Willard's voiceover for Francis Ford Coppola's *Apocalypse Now* (1979), whose world-weary cynicism – while echoing Conrad's *Heart of Darkness* (1899), on which Coppola's film was loosely based – carries with it more than a hint of Fowler's own. Mankiewicz's film appears to have had a similar catalytic effect. Although Jean-Luc Godard's notorious claim that *The Quiet American* was the best film of 1958 – a year that also saw released Alfred Hitchcock's *Vertigo*, Ingmar Bergman's *Wild Strawberries* and the Orson Welles vehicle *Touch of Evil* – is perhaps stretching things, it has had a lasting and important influence of its own. As Neil Sinyard has pointed out, it 'anticipates a number of war films of the 1980s' – notably Peter Weir's *The Year of Living Dangerously* (1982), Roger Spottiswoode's *Under Fire* (1983), Roland Joffe's *The Killing Fields* (1984) and Oliver Stone's *Salvador* (1985) – 'where the leading protagonist is not a combatant but a journalist, who starts just by taking pictures but ends up taking sides' (Sinyard, 2003, p. 152). Mankiewicz's decision to make Pyle an ultimately guileless, guiltless victim may have incensed Greene. Yet although Pyle is no longer facilitating terrorism in the name of US-style democracy, the film remains in its exploration of the involvement of the United States in world affairs one of the more surprising and challenging films to have emerged from 1950s Hollywood.

What view Greene might have taken of the 2002 film of *The Quiet American*, scripted by Christopher Hampton and directed by Phillip Noyce, is a matter of intriguing speculation, especially given his long-standing antipathy towards Mankiewicz's film. If Mankiewicz's film shows an attentiveness to the novel in its use of much of Greene's original dialogue, where Noyce and Hampton stick closely to the novel, and diverge from the preceding film, is in their full restoration of Pyle's guilt. In their version, Pyle is revealed 'to be the virtual mastermind behind everything: a CIA kingpin whose fresh-faced Ivy League mask falls away at the end to reveal a coldly ideological functionary. It is a very strong moment, in excess of the more elusive persona proposed by Greene' (Bradshaw, 2002). In the novel, Pyle is anatomized by Fowler thus: 'With his gangly legs and his crew-cut and his wide campus gaze' – recalling 'Audie Murphy's brand of earnest all-Americanness' in the 1958 film (Falk, 2000, p. 99) – 'he seemed incapable of harm' (*QA*, p. 9). In the 2002 film, Pyle (played by the Canadian actor Brendan Fraser) wears spectacles and a pale suit, details 'which explicitly recall 60s defence secretary Robert McNamara, the technocratic Albert Speer of the Vietnam war' (Patterson, 2002) – a conflict that, for many critics, Greene's novel foresaw. The addition of spectacles may also be a concession to the Pyle depicted by Greene, who towards the end of the novel confesses to being 'as blind as a coot' (*QA*, p. 170), a revelation which, given the narrative's insistence on Pyle's lack of political intuition or insight, carries a particularly heavy irony. In Conrad's *Heart of Darkness*, the narrator famously characterizes the European imperialisms of the nineteenth-century – 'the old colonial powers' dismissed by Pyle (*QA*, p. 115) – as 'men going at it blind'. Perhaps Greene had in mind this image from his predecessor Conrad's most celebrated work for his criticism, through Pyle, of the *Pax Americana* of the mid-twentieth century.

The old imperialist Fowler, meanwhile, has not only seen it all before, but has also seen what is coming. Noyce's film closes with a montage of newspaper headlines which proleptically reveal the escalation of American involvement in Vietnam. As well as underscoring the prophetic power of Greene's novel, this series of images also recalls Fowler's journalistic tendency in the novel to think 'in headlines', as his response to Pyle's demise illustrates: 'I was a correspondent: I thought in headlines. "American official murdered in Saigon"' (*QA*, p. 13). When put in the context of the closing headlines of Noyce's adaptation, Fowler's words assume a bigger political and historical dimension, the murdered figure of Pyle becoming in retrospect the first US casualty of the later American war. Noyce's motivation for keeping to the original plot can be seen to reflect a particular set of personal and cultural circumstances, as much as stemming from any desire to revisit and restore the political vision of the novel effaced by Mankiewicz's film. Noyce belongs to the generation of Australians pressed into military service in Vietnam during the 1960s and early 1970s, as a result of the same fears over the spread of communism in Southeast Asia – the so-called 'domino' theory – rehearsed and rejected by Fowler in the novel: '"I know the record. Siam goes. Malaya goes. Indonesia goes"' (*QA*, p. 86).

Noyce's adaptation also had an unintended contemporary political resonance, which saw its release considerably delayed. The $40 million production was shelved following the 11 September 2001 attacks on the World Trade Center in New York City, having only had its rough-cut preview the day before (Thompson, 2002). This was because those involved in marketing and promoting the film felt that it risked undermining the nascent 'war on terror', as it proposes an American foreign policy that is involved in sponsoring overseas terrorism. Clearly, and to the detriment of its prospects of securing a theatrical release, the film's distributors unfortunately shared Fowler's tendency to think 'in headlines'. The principle '"Isms" and "ocracies"' anatomized by Fowler in the novel, Communism and Democracy (*QA*, 87), had been supplanted by another set of antagonistic worldviews, 'Terror' and 'Freedom', and in this context of renewed American patriotism at home and political uncertainty abroad, the anti-Americanism associated with Greene in general, and with the source novel in particular, no doubt little helped matters. As such, although it was filmed in 2001, the film was not released in cinemas until late 2002. *The Quiet American* opened to general acclaim – in particular for Michael Caine's performance as Fowler, which Caine later described as 'among my best work' (Caine, 2011, p. 382). There is a certain symmetry to the fact that Caine, who made his first major film appearance in the 1964 imperialist yarn *Zulu*, should save one of his most acclaimed later performances for the role of an 'anti-hero' (p. 316) embittered with the imperial project.

In an interview publicizing the film, Caine claimed to have based his 'portrayal of Fowler on Greene himself': 'I just copied something of the way he spoke, and his movements. They were very small movements. Journalists are like policemen, they're always looking for things; their eyes go around all over the place, over your shoulder to see what's happening' (*View London*, 2002). For critics such as Philip French, Caine's performance channels not only Greene, but also a little too much of the *Ipcress File*'s Harry Palmer, the role that made him famous (French, 2002). Nonetheless, Caine here pinpoints an essential component of Greene's journalism and fiction: the watchfulness that informs composition. This was famously outlined by Greene in his first foray into autobiography, *A Sort of Life* (1971). Greene recollects being on the lookout for material while laid up in hospital following an appendectomy: 'There is a splinter of ice in the heart of a writer. I watched and listened. This was something which one day I might need' (*A Sort of Life*, p. 134).

Moreover, by suggestively playing Fowler *as* Greene, Caine indirectly gestures to the critical tendency which has seen Fowler's views – in particular his unabashed anti-Americanism – interpreted as Greene's own. In a letter to Evelyn Waugh from 4 January 1961, Greene refers to such a manoeuvre as one of 'the old-time gag[s]' of literary criticism (R. Greene, 2007, p. 252). It can certainly be problematic to identify an author with his characters – not least with Greene, who always insisted on there being a necessary distance between the two, as his claim in the prefatory note to *The Quiet American* that 'Pyle, Granger, Fowler, Vigot, Joe [...] have had no originals in the life of Saigon or Hanoi' underlines. Yet there is also some substance to such a comparison. Bendrix in *The End of the Affair* and Querry in *A Burnt-Out Case*, in particular, each possess shades of Greene. Equally, Fowler's opinion of the war in Vietnam bears more than a passing resemblance to Greene's own, as his autobiographical writings, journalism and essays on the subject reflect. For example, in *Ways of Escape* Greene describes 'my ambivalent attitude to the war [...] my admiration for the French army, my admiration for their enemies [the communist Viet Minh], and my doubt of any final value in the war' (*WE*, p. 157). Greene's description here of the life-long 'spell' cast upon him by Vietnam also recalls 'the real background' which so mesmerizes Fowler in the novel: 'the tall elegant girls in white silk trousers [...] the pewter evening light on flat paddy fields [...] the French perfumeries in the rue Catinat, the Chinese gambling houses in Cholon [...] that feeling of exhilaration which a measure of danger brings' (*WE*, p. 154). A fondness for a game of *quatre cent vingt-et-un* and for smoking 'a little opium' (pp. 158–9) add to a small but compelling list of consonances between character and creator.

Michael Redgrave had seen the chance to play Fowler as a great opportunity, one that might even bring an Oscar, describing it as 'Just about the best part' to be had in 1958 (Redgrave, 1983, p. 213, p. 247). Caine had picked up an Oscar for his role at the hub of another love triangle in Woody Allen's *Hannah and Her Sisters* (1987), and was again nominated at the 2003 Academy Awards for his performance as Fowler. However, Caine's Oscar chances were hindered by much the same problem of timing as that which beset the film's eventual US release. As Caine explains in his autobiography, *The Elephant to Hollywood* (2011): 'A lot of show business is about timing and in this instance the timing was against *The Quiet American*': 'The Americans invaded Iraq on 20 March 2003; the Academy Awards were just four days later on 24 March' (Caine, 2011, p. 327). Oscar or no Oscar, Caine felt that, having earlier starred in the somewhat underwhelming film of Greene's *The Honorary Consul* in 1983, *The Quiet American* had at least, and at last, provided him with the 'chance to make a film of a Graham Greene novel that the author, who is one of my favourites, would have been proud of' (p. 316).

In the novel Pyle is given to espousing his political vision of a Vietnam 'free' from Western interference and 'the taint of colonialism' (*QA*, p. 115). This attitude is ironic not only given the massive escalation of America's presence in Vietnam in the years following the novel's publication, but also in the context of Noyce and Hampton's adaptation, whose release coincided with the American invasions of Iraq and Afghanistan. The film's eventual release in 2002 also coincided with that of Francis Ford Coppola's *Apocalypse Now Redux*, the 'director's cut' of his 1979 Vietnam War epic, whose famous opening Noyce's film pays homage to through 'a nightmarish superimposition of flames, explosions and distorted faces' (French, 2002), and whose 'dark interiors, blindingly white daytime streets' and 'humid, menacing countryside' (French, 2002) provide an archetypal vision of war-torn Vietnam upon which Noyce's film also draws. Interestingly, Coppola's *Redux* version reinstates the previously cut 'French plantation scene', thus implicitly connecting the French and American involvements in Southeast Asia. After all, from a Vietnamese perspective these wars can be seen as belonging to the same history of Western imperialism and intervention – an equivalence that Greene's novel also draws when Fowler points out to Pyle that, to the Vietnamese, he is effectively 'a European too' (*QA*, p. 87). Tellingly, Noyce's film was warmly received in Vietnam, not only for economic reasons as the first Hollywood film to be made almost entirely on location in the country (for its detailed recreation of early 1950s Saigon and Hanoi), but also for sharing the novel's nuanced, 'long view' of Western involvement in the country. The fact that Noyce and Hampton also keep closely to Greene's novel – which, as Caine notes, today has an 'almost iconic status' in Vietnam (Caine, 2011, p. 320) – no doubt also helped the film's favourable reception there.

As films produced by and for the Hollywood mainstream, both the 1958 and the 2002 adaptations are unusual in treading a fine and frequently provocative line as works that, like the novel, explore the politics of the burgeoning role of the United States as the 'world's policeman'. To say this is an uncomfortable issue for either the Hollywood of the McCarthyist 1950s or the post-Vietnam, post-11 September era, would be a huge understatement. This power to unsettle and provoke debate demonstrates the abiding significance of Greene's novel, then as now. If anything, the fraught global political context into which Noyce's film was released underscores 'Greene's continuing, extraordinary relevance as we gingerly assimilate and evaluate today's new world order' (Sinyard, 2003, p. 160). This in turn underlines the extent to which Greene's novels have long been, and will long remain, a key resource for film adapters, for continuing to colour how we view the world.

Exercises

- It is interesting that Greene's novel *The Quiet American* – so often regarded as thoroughly anti-American – was twice selected by Hollywood as a source. Having read the novel and seen the films, can you assess what was and remains the appeal of this provocative novel for the film industry?
- Consider *The Quiet American* in relation to other films that explore the place of the United States in global politics. Films about the Vietnam War are particularly relevant, but you may like to consider fact-based films such as *A Mighty Heart* (Michael Winterbottom, 2007), about the kidnapping of an American journalist in Pakistan, or *Captain Phillips* (Paul Greengrass, 2013), about the commandeering of a vessel by Somali pirates.
- Consider the options available to a novelist or filmmaker when merging fact and fiction. In addition, how do the aspects of drama and performance come into play when adapting a novel?
- One of the most acclaimed Vietnam War films, *Apocalypse Now*, is closely modelled on a distinctive, classic text which it 're-locates' into a different context. *The Quiet American* is a powerful evocation of a particular time and place. Could the underlying story and the plot of *The Quiet American* be 're-presented' in a different locale and era? How would you approach this?

Conclusion

Graham Greene produced a richly diverse collection of fiction, highly distinctive while at the same time drawing heavily upon generic convention. His stories remain by turns timeless in their themes and yet simultaneously evocative of their cultural moment, capturing tumultuous episodes of twentieth-century history both in Britain and across the globe: from the violence of gangland Brighton between the wars to the inner life of London at war, from economic opportunism in post-war Vienna to the mounting conflict in colonial Vietnam and, beyond this, the displacement of the old imperialisms of Europe by the new globalism of the United States. But places are nothing without people: from Pinkie Brown to Sarah Miles, to Harry Lime or Alden Pyle, Greene created extraordinary, hauntingly lasting figures to populate these narratives. In his fiction, as in his travel writing and journalism, Greene brought to his readers vivid portrayals of the worlds he explored and saw around him: these may have become history to us now, but the dramatic dynamic of his characters and situations continue to resonate and come alive with each reading and with each new generation of readers – many of whom are as likely to have encountered Greene through adaptations of his novels for the screen as through the novels themselves.

Greene is one of the first British authors to be influenced by cinema. He was schooled in the art of the screen first as a film-lover and reviewer, and later as a screenwriter, and this leaves its mark on his fiction: in terms of its evocative power and economy of style, all of Greene's fiction is to some degree 'cinematic'. That is not to say there is a facile quality to his work: Greene was thoroughly a novelist, not a frustrated filmmaker. Nor is his fiction, though cinematic, always *already suited* to adaptation. Greene's novels and short stories may all have cinematic potential, but they will always test any adapter. After all, the masterpieces of Greene adaptation are outweighed by works that are, at best, 'could have beens' – and by those that are very far from either category. Some of these adaptations are classics of cinema that have stood the test of time (*The Third Man*), some were acclaimed on their release but are now neglected (*The Fallen Idol*), and some that were overlooked then are undergoing revaluation now (Mankiewicz's *The Quiet American*).

As we have touched upon, reception is, to a significant degree, historically relative. Unlike his literary forebears James, Ford and Conrad, and despite his early experiment with narrative form in *The Man Within* (1929), Greene never saw himself as a modernist writer (Barrett, 2009, p. 423). Yet his literary works unarguably engaged with that most modernist of technologies, cinema, and it is the films that are seen to be overtly modernist, either in outlook or aesthetic, which continue to resonate with critics, then as now – most obviously Greene and Reed's *The Third Man*. Equally, Greene's works are often suffused with an acute sense of their wider cultural, historical or political contexts, and it is because of this that some have gone on to become modern classics. It is for similar reasons that films of his works that were overlooked at the time of their initial release, such as Mankiewicz's *The Quiet American*, have undergone revaluation for their new-found geo-political astuteness in the years since the Cold War.

From his earliest works onward, Greene's fiction has attracted filmmakers, but as these shifting critical fortunes imply, the process of adaptation has not always been without its challenges. It is precisely these challenges that make the dual process of reading his fiction and watching the numerous attempts to film it such a rewarding enterprise. Central to this process are some key issues for us to consider:

- What do Greene's novels 'give' to the filmmaker? Characters and locations? Dialogue and descriptions? Conflicts and passions?
- What are the challenges his novels pose for the adapter? Irony and interiority? Scope and situation? The narrative voice and its relationship to the individual reader?
- How have filmmakers interpreted Greene's fiction through the years? How have they used Greene as a source text to create works that are not only entertaining but also of continued historical or cultural relevance?
- We should also not be afraid to consider how we might adapt Greene ourselves. How might we use Greene's fiction to throw light on our own time, locale or situation? To this end, you might wish to consider some of his less-known works as well as his better-known ones.

Although it is his engagement with cinema that tends to dominate discussion of Greene and adaptation, we should not overlook some of the other media to which Greene's fiction has lent itself. As an author, Greene's critical reputation and popular legacy rests mainly on his novels, but he was also a short story writer of considerable skill and dexterity. In the 1970s, Thames Television produced *Shades of Greene* (1975–6), a television series featuring dramatizations of some of Greene's most accomplished short fiction, adapted by notable writers such as William Trevor, Clive Exton, Robin Chapman and John Mortimer. These one-hour television plays had high production values (in contrast to some of the films of Greene's works such as *The Human Factor*), and starred celebrated British actors including John Gielgud, Denholm Elliot, John Hurt, Eleanor Bron, Ian Hendry, Arthur Lowe and Michael Gough. *Shades of Greene* ran to 18 episodes over two series, and its longevity partly stems from the fact that Greene's short fiction spans a wide range of genres suitable for popular television: from the horror story 'A Little Place Off the Edgware Road' to the comic work of irony and innuendo 'The Blue Film', to the tale of colonial adventurism in Africa, 'A Chance for Mr Lever'. The 1970s was arguably the golden era for episodic television drama in Britain, and *Shades of Greene* can be situated alongside contemporary television series such as Nigel Kneale's *Beasts* (1976) and Brian Clemens's *Thriller* (1973–6): all are stand-alone dramas with well-crafted scripts, high production values and talented actors. In particular, *Shades of Greene* can be seen as a precursor to the hugely popular series of Roald Dahl adaptations, *Tales of the Unexpected* (1979–88), which, like *Shades of Greene*, encompassed the macabre and the comic in equal, and similarly gleeful, measure.

Like Greene himself, *Shades of Greene* was occasionally controversial. The final episode of the first series, 'The Destructors' – based on Greene's 1954 short story of the same title – aired in October 1975. It was scripted by John Mortimer and directed by Michael Apted. It is about a gang of teenagers who break into a house while the owner is away and proceed systematically to dismantle it, leaving a shell which collapses before the returning owner's eyes. One of Greene's most compelling short stories, this narrative of disaffected youths committing an act of sustained sadism with military precision was a powerful metaphor for post-war Britain, and bore comparison with William Golding's novel *Lord of the Flies* (1954) and Edward Bond's equally controversial play *Saved* (1965). The cast of teenage actors – including the young Phil Daniels – gave the adaptation a powerful authenticity that shocked viewers at the time. As Norman Sherry reveals, the broadcast provoked a flood of complaints and a corresponding outrage in the national press, where it was 'described as wicked, corrupt and frightening' (Sherry, 1994, p. 66) – echoing the fictional outrage provoked by the story's use as a school text in Richard Kelly's 2001 film *Donnie Darko*. 'The Destructors' is an outwardly simple story that still has the power to disturb, with its representation of children committing a concerted, collective – and above all, coldly pitiless – act of brutality, and, as the reaction to it suggests, the *Shades of Greene* adaptation is highly effective in channelling this. Greene's story has since taken on a life of its own as an adaptive source, from amateur adaptations using live actors to computer animations using Lego on video-sharing sites such as YouTube.

In addition to the visual media of film, television and theatre (several of Greene's novels have been adapted for the stage), it is also worth remembering that Greene's works have regularly been adapted for radio; in fact, much of his fiction has through the years either been read aloud or dramatized for the airwaves. In some regards, the complex narrative strategies and richly articulated characters in Greene's works find an advantage in audio dramatization. Particularly noteworthy examples include Gregory Evans's three-part version of *The Quiet American*, starring Ian Holm as Fowler, which was broadcast in 1990, and Rene Basilico's five-part version of *Travels With My Aunt*, starring the popular female impersonator Dame Hilda Bracket (Patrick Fyffe) as the indomitable Aunt Augusta, which was broadcast in 1997.

Just as Greene's fiction has been adapted to countless different media, so, too, are its possibilities for adaptation seemingly limitless. The map of the world may have been redrawn in the decades since Greene's death in 1991, but the themes of corruption, crisis, betrayal and redemption throughout his works continue to be relevant and viable as adaptive sources. For instance, the post-war horrors of economic exploitation represented in *The Third Man* are suggestively adaptable to any other zone of post-war crisis or natural disaster. Similarly, although location seems compelled by *Brighton Rock*, the 2010 film version proves that historical period is not. In the near century since he began to write, Greene has moved from being an author of genre fiction to an author of modern classics, and his current standing is due in no small part to his continuing relevance through the years, and this relevance in turn feeds, and is fed by, the adaptation of those works.

Despite the simple clarity of his prose, Greene is not always the 'easiest' of authors. Yet his powerful themes, strong characterization and evocative landscapes – whether psychological or physical – have long appealed, and will continue to appeal, to successive generations of audiences. Greene had tales worth telling and numerous adapters, so different in their own right, have been drawn to the challenge of metamorphosing his stories into and through different media. Doubtless, this will continue. Just as his works will continue to reach and reward new generations of readers, so, too, will the adaptation of his works – whether for cinema or television, or audio or digital media – continue to make Greene come alive in different and dynamic ways on each new experience of reception.

Works Cited

Unless otherwise stated, all references to Graham Greene's works are to the Vintage Classics edition (London: Vintage) 2004–11.

Adamson, Judith (1984) *Graham Greene and Cinema* (Norman, OK: Pilgrim Books).

Allain, Marie-Françoise (ed.) (1983) *The Other Man: Conversations with Graham Greene*, trans. Guido Waldman (London: Bodley Head).

Barrett, Dorothea (2009) 'Graham Greene' in Adrian Poole (ed.) *The Cambridge Companion to English Novelists* (Cambridge: Cambridge University Press).

Bergonzi, Bernard (2006) *A Study in Greene: Graham Greene and the Art of the Novel* (Oxford: Oxford University Press).

BFI (1949) '*The Third Man* Pressbook', Pressbooks Collection, British Film Institute Library, London.

Bowen, Marjorie (2004) *The Viper of Milan* (London: Elliott and Thompson).

Bowser, Eileen (1990) *The Transformation of Cinema, 1907–1915* (Oakland, CA: University of California Press).

Bradshaw, Peter (2002) 'The Quiet American', *Guardian*, 28 November, http://theguardian.com (home page), date accessed 6 March 2012.

Brennan, Michael G. (2010) *Graham Greene: Fictions, Faith and Authorship* (London: Continuum).

Brooke, Michael (2010) 'The Hays Code', BFI Screenonline, http://www.screenonline.org.uk (home page), date accessed 19 July 2010.

Buchan, John (1916) *The Power-House* (Edinburgh: Blackwood).

Caine, Michael (2011) *The Elephant to Hollywood* (London: Hodder & Stoughton).

Cartmell, Deborah and Whelehan, Imelda (eds) (2007) *The Cambridge Companion to Literature on Screen* (Cambridge: Cambridge University Press).

Cartmell, Deborah and Whelehan, Imelda (2010) *Screen Adaptation: Impure Cinema* (Basingstoke: Palgrave Macmillan).

Chibnall, Steve (2006) *Brighton Rock* (London: I. B. Tauris).

Coroneos, Con (2002) *Space, Conrad, and Modernity* (Oxford: Oxford University Press).

Cowie, Peter (1973) *A Ribbon of Dreams: The Cinema of Orson Welles* (New York: Da Capo).

Davis, Ronald L. (1997) *John Ford: Hollywood's Old Master* (Norman, OK: University of Oklahoma Press).

Donaghy, Henry J. (ed.) (1992) *Conversations with Graham Greene* (Jackson, MS: University Press of Mississippi).

Drazin, Charles (2000) *In Search of the Third Man* (London: Methuen).

Dunning, John (1998) *On the Air: The Encyclopedia of Old-Time Radio* (Oxford: Oxford University Press).

Duràn, Leopoldo (1994) *Graham Greene: Friend and Brother*, trans. Euan Cameron (London: HarperCollins).

Durgnat, Raymond (1974) *The Strange Case of Alfred Hitchcock* (London: Methuen).

Eagleton, Terry (2007) 'Adventures in Greene-land', *Guardian*, 22 September, http://theguardian.com (home page), date accessed 27 April 2012.

Evans, Peter William (2005) *Carol Reed* (Manchester: Manchester University Press).

Falk, Quentin (2000) *Travels in Greeneland: The Complete Guide to the Cinema of Graham Greene* (London: Reynolds & Hearn).

Feigel, Lara and Harris, Alexandra (eds) (2009) *Modernism on Sea: Art and Culture at the British Seaside* (Witney: Peter Lang).

Foden, Giles (2000) 'Sad-eyed chronicler of sex and sin', *Guardian*, 7 January, http://theguardian.com (home page), date accessed 27 April 2012.

French, Philip (2000) 'Bitter and Twisting', *Observer*, 13 February, http://the guardian.com (home page), date accessed 16 April 2012.

French, Philip (2002) 'Pastures Greene', *Observer*, 1 December, http://theguardian.com (home page), date accessed 6 March 2012.

French, Philip (2008) 'The Quiet American', *Observer*, 14 September, http://theguardian.com (home page), date accessed 6 March 2012.

Gillan, Audrey (2000) 'End of Affair stars attack "hypocrisy"', *Guardian*, 1 February, http://theguardian.com (home page), date accessed 16 January 2012.

Greene, Graham (1980) *The Pleasure-Dome: The Collected Film Criticism, 1935–1940*, ed. John Russell Taylor (Oxford: Oxford University Press).

Greene, Richard (ed.) (2007) *Graham Greene: A Life in Letters* (London: Little, Brown).

Guardian (2000a) 'Has the British Film Censor lost all sense of proportion?', 5 February, http://theguardian.com (home page), date accessed 16 June 2014.

Guardian (2000b) 'Guardian Interviews at the BFI', 4 February, http://the guardian.com (home page), date accessed 16 June 2014.

Hand, Richard J. (2010) '"It must all change now!": Victor Hugo's *Lucretia Borgia* and Adaptation Practices in Theatre' in Dennis Cutchins, Laurence Raw and James M. Welsh (eds) *Redefining Adaptation Studies* (Lanham, MD: Scarecrow Press).

Herr, Michael (1978) *Dispatches* (London: Picador).

Higham, Charles (1971) *The Films of Orson Welles* (Berkeley, CA: University of California Press).

Holloway, Mark (1976) *Norman Douglas: A Biography* (London: Secker and Warburg).

Hoskins, Robert (1999) *Graham Greene: An Approach to the Novels* (London: Routledge).

Hutcheon, Linda (2006) *A Theory of Adaptation* (London: Routledge).

Hynes, Samuel L. (ed.) (1973) *Graham Greene: A Collection of Critical Essays* (Englewood Cliffs, NJ: Prentice-Hall).

Kael, Pauline (1965) *Kiss Kiss Bang Bang* (Boston, MA: Little, Brown).

Karl, Frederick R. and Davies, Laurence (eds) (1983) *The Collected Letters of Joseph Conrad, Volume 1: 1861–1897* (Cambridge: Cambridge University Press).

Korda, Michael (1999) *Another Life: A Memoir of Other People* (New York: Random House).

Kulshrestha, J. P. (1977) *Graham Greene: The Novelist* (Delhi: Macmillan in India).

Leitch, Thomas (2003) 'Twelve Fallacies in Contemporary Adaptation Theory', *Criticism*, 45.2, 149–71.

Leitch, Thomas (2008) 'Adaptation Studies at a Cross-Roads', *Adaptation*, 1.1, 63–77.

Lodge, David (2005) 'Foreword', *No Man's Land* (London: Hesperus).

Lodge, David (2006) 'Did the butler do it?', *Guardian*, 4 November, http://theguardian.com (home page), date accessed 11 June 2014.

McFarlane, Brian (ed.) (2005) *The Encyclopedia of British Cinema* (London: Methuen).

Minier, Márta (2014) 'Definitions, Dyads, Triads and Other Points of Connection in Translation and Adaptation Discourse' in Katja Krebs (ed.) *Translation and Adaptation in Theatre and Film* (London: Routledge).

Moore, Gene M. (1996) 'Conrad's Influence' in J. H. Stape (ed.) *The Cambridge Companion to Joseph Conrad* (Cambridge: Cambridge University Press).

Mudford, Peter (1996) *Graham Greene* (Tavistock: Northcote House).

Napper, Lawrence (2000) 'British Cinema and the Middlebrow' in Justine Ashby and Andrew Higson (eds) *British Cinema, Past and Present* (London: Routledge).

Nashel, Jonathan (1996) 'Lansdale and Greene' in John Clark Pratt (ed.) *The Quiet American: Text and Criticism* (New York: Penguin).

Orwell, George (1973) 'The Sanctified Sinner' in Samuel L. Hynes (ed.) *Graham Greene: A Collection of Critical Essays* (Englewood Cliffs, NJ: Prentice-Hall).

Parkinson, Graham (ed.) (1993) *Mornings in the Dark: The Graham Greene Film Reader: Reviews, Essays, Interviews and Film Stories* (New York: Applause).

Patterson, John (2002) 'Greene on the Screen', *Guardian*, 15 November, http://theguardian.com (home page), date accessed 6 March 2012.

Pendleton, Robert (1996) *Graham Greene's Conradian Masterplot: The Arabesques of Influence* (Basingstoke: Macmillan, 1996).

Phelps, Guy (1997) 'Britain: Out of Fear and Ignorance' in Ruth Petrie (ed.) *Film and Censorship: the Index Reader* (London: Cassell).

Pratt, John Clark (1996) 'Introduction', John Clark Pratt (ed.) *The Quiet American: Text and Criticism* (New York: Penguin).

Pryce-Jones, David (1973) *Graham Greene* (Edinburgh: Oliver and Boyd).

Queenan, Joe (2002) 'Raising Caine', *Guardian*, 30 November, http://theguardian.com (home page), date accessed 6 March 2012.

Redgrave, Michael (1983) *In My Mind's Eye: An Autobiography* (London: Weidenfeld & Nicolson).

Said, Edward (1994) *Culture and Imperialism* (New York: Vintage Books).

Samuels, Charles Thomas (1972) *Encountering Directors* (New York: Capricorn).

Sanders, Julie (2006) *Adaptation and Appropriation* (London: Routledge).

Seed, David (2005) 'British Modernists Encounter the Cinema' in David Seed (ed.) *Literature and the Visual Media: Essays and Studies* (Cambridge: D. S. Brewer).

Sexton, James (2005) 'Introduction', *No Man's Land* (London: Hesperus).

Shelden, Michael (1994) *Graham Greene: The Man Within* (London: Random House).

Sherry, Norman (1989) *The Life of Graham Greene: Volume One, 1904–1939* (London: Jonathan Cape).

Sherry, Norman (1994) *The Life of Graham Greene: Volume Two, 1939–1955* (London: Jonathan Cape).

Sherry, Norman (2004) *The Life of Graham Greene: Volume Three, 1955–1991* (London: Jonathan Cape).

Sinyard, Neil (2003) *Graham Greene: A Literary Life* (Basingstoke: Palgrave Macmillan).

Smith, Zadie (2004) 'Introduction', *The Quiet American* (London: Vintage).

Spurling, John (1983) *Graham Greene* (London: Methuen).

Stam, Robert and Raengo, Alessandra (eds) (2004) *A Companion to Literature and Film* (Malden: Blackwell).

Stapleton, Michael (1983) *The Cambridge Guide to English Literature* (Cambridge: Cambridge University Press).

Theroux, Paul (2005) 'Introduction', *The Comedians* (New York: Penguin).

Thompson, Anne (2002) 'Films with War Themes Are Victims of Bad Timing', *New York Times*, 17 October, http://nytimes.com (home page), date accessed 17 June 2014.

Thomson, Brian Lindsay (2009) *Graham Greene and the Politics of Popular Fiction and Film* (London: Palgrave Macmillan).

Tóibín, Colm (2005) 'Introduction', *The Human Factor* (London: Vintage).

View London (2002) 'Michael Caine Interview', http://www.viewlondon.co.uk (home page), date accessed 26 March 2012.

Walsh, Nick Paton (1999) 'Graham Greene's screen alter egos', *Observer*, 27 June, http://theguardian.com (home page), date accessed 27 April 2012.

Watts, Cedric Thomas (1997) *A Preface to Greene* (Harlow: Longman).

Welles, Orson and Bogdanovich, Peter (1993) *This is Orson Welles*, ed. Jonathan Rosenbaum (London: HarperCollins).

White, Rob (2012a) '*The Third Man*: Critical Reception', BFI Screenonline, http://www.screenonline.org.uk (home page), date accessed 24 January 2013.

White, Rob (2012b) 'The Origins of *The Third Man*', BFI Screenonline, http://www.screenonline.org.uk (home page), date accessed 30 January 2013.

White, Rob (2012c) 'Adapting *The Third Man*', BFI Screenonline, http://www.screenonline.org.uk (home page), date accessed 24 January 2013.

Wyndham, Francis (1958) *Graham Greene* (London: British Council and the National Book League).

Zabel, Morton D. (1948) 'Graham Greene' in W. V. O'Connor (ed.) *Forms of Modern Fiction* (Minneapolis, MN: University of Minnesota Press).

Select filmography

This list features a selection of the Graham Greene film adaptations discussed. A highly detailed list is available at the Internet Movie Database (http://www. imdb.com) and at the BFI Film and TV Database (http://old.bfi.org.uk/filmtvinfo/ ftvdb/). In addition, a helpful annotated filmography is available in Sinyard (2003), pp. 143–60.

Brighton Rock (US title: *Young Scarface*) (John Boulting, 1947)
Brighton Rock (Rowan Joffe, 2010)
The Comedians (Peter Glenville, 1967)
The End of the Affair (Edward Dmytryk, 1955)
The End of the Affair (Neil Jordan, 1999)
England Made Me (Peter Duffell, 1972)
The Fallen Idol (based on 'The Basement Room', 1935) (Carol Reed, 1948)
The Fugitive (based on *The Power and the Glory*, 1940) (John Ford, 1947)
The Green Cockatoo (a.k.a. *Race Gang*) (William Cameron Menzies, 1937)
This Gun For Hire (based on *A Gun for Sale*, 1936) (Frank Tuttle, 1941)
The Heart of the Matter (George More O'Ferrall, 1953)
The Honorary Consul (John Mackenzie, 1983)
The Human Factor (Otto Preminger, 1979)
Loser Takes All (Ken Annakin, 1956)
The Man Within (US title: *The Smugglers*) (Bernard Knowles, 1947)
Ministry of Fear (Fritz Lang, 1944)
Orient Express (based on *Stamboul Train*, 1932) (Paul Martin, 1934)
Our Man in Havana (Carol Reed, 1959)
The Quiet American (Joseph L. Mankiewicz, 1958)
The Quiet American (Phillip Noyce, 2002)
The Stranger's Hand (Mario Soldati, 1954)

The Third Man (Carol Reed, 1949)
Travels with My Aunt (George Cukor, 1972)
Went the Day Well? (based on 'The Lieutenant Died Last', 1940) (Alberto Cavalcanti, 1942)

Select television and radio adaptations

Full details of television series can be found at the BFI Film and TV Database (http://old.bfi.org.uk/filmtvinfo/ftvdb/).

The Quiet American (BBC radio series, 1990).
Shades of Greene (Thames Television series, 1975–6).
The Third Man (BBC radio version, 1950).
The Third Man (BBC radio version, 1959).
The Third Man (BBC radio version, 1971).
The Third Man (BBC television series, 1959–65).
The Third Man (*Lux Radio Theater* radio version, 1951).
The Third Man (*Lux Radio Theater* radio version, 1954).
The Third Man (*United States Steel Hour* radio version, 1951).
The Third Man: The Adventures of Harry Lime (BBC radio series, 1951–2).
Travels with My Aunt (BBC radio series, 1997).

Index

145

CPSIA information can be obtained
at www.ICGtesting.com
Printed in the USA
BVHW040219210820
586971BV00012B/94